Uniforms & Equipment of the British Army in World War I

Uniforms & Equipment of the British Army in World War I

A Study in Period Photographs

ROYAL FLYING CORPS • FIELD INFANTRY • MGC AND TANK CORPS • ROYAL ENGINEERS • ROYAL ARTILLERY • INFANTRY WEAPONS • INSIGNIA •

Stephen J. Chambers

Schiffer Military History
Atglen, PA

Acknowledgements

I could not have written this book without the help of a number of people who have not only given up their time to lend knowledge and advice, but have kindly given permission to include photographs from their collections.

Special thanks must go firstly to Andrew Read and Guy Marner. Andy kindly offered a superb choice of images from his photographic archive, and also shared his detailed knowledge of the subject. Guy should also be thanked for the photographs loaned, most importantly those relating to the air force, and his in-depth knowledge, all of which has proved to be invaluable. Thanks must also go to Steve Farrant and Andrew Tonge who both kindly gave permission to use images from their collections. Lastly thanks to Michael Forbes-Ford who spent his time carefully reading the proofs, and to the team at Schiffer, especially Bob Biondi for his patience and support. I must finally thank my wife, Joanne. Her loving support, encouragement and understanding, during a time when our home was swamped with photographs and books, have helped make this all possible.

Stephen Chambers
West Sussex, January 2005
E-mail: steve.chambers@dsl.pipex.com

Book design by Robert Biondi.

Library of Congress Catalog Number: 2004111120.

Printed in China.
ISBN: 0-7643-2154-4

Published by Schiffer Publishing Ltd.
4880 Lower Valley Road
Atglen, PA 19310
Phone: (610) 593-1777
FAX: (610) 593-2002
E-mail: Info@schifferbooks.com.
Visit our web site at: www.schifferbooks.com
Please write for a free catalog.
This book may be purchased from the publisher.
Please include $3.95 postage.
Try your bookstore first.

In Europe, Schiffer books are distributed by:
Bushwood Books
6 Marksbury Ave.
Kew Gardens
Surrey TW9 4JF
England
Phone: 44 (0)20 8392-8585
FAX: 44 (0)20 8392-9876
E-mail: Bushwd@aol.com.
Free postage in the UK. Europe: air mail at cost.
Try your bookstore first.

Contents

Introduction

One of the best ways to illustrate the wide variety of uni forms and equipment used by the British Army between 1900 and 1918 is through contemporary photographs. Following on from Charles Woolley's excellent books on the Imperial German Army, an obvious gap existed that needed filling on a photographic history of the British Army during the same period.

There are many books published on the British Army during this period, but none using contemporary photographs as a study of the uniforms and equipment. Each photograph has a short and informative caption, but at the end of the day *a picture is worth a thousand words*. Most of the images shown were taken on active service, in the many small towns and villages that were scattered close to the frontline. Quality photographs of this nature are now very rare, and have been brought together by many years of collecting to best illustrate to the historian, collector, re-enactor, modeller and general military enthusiast, the variations of uniform and equipment used during this period. The book does not show each and every individual piece of clothing, equipment, insignia or unit of the British Army, but hopefully gives an enriched selection of the most common, as well as some of the most unusual, items of field kit that were in use at the turn of the 20th Century.

• • •

Military and armed conflicts attracted photographers from the earliest years. The Crimean War of 1854 gave the world the first known war photographers. The two pioneers of this art were the Englishman, Roger Fenton, and the lesser-known Rumanian named Karol de Szathmari. Both showed the world, arguably the first photographic images of war. Formally mounted portrait photographs, taken against artistic cloth backings, were made in the form of *Carte de Visite* (CDV) and Cabinet Cards. These were mounted on cardboard stiffeners and given to family, friends and loved ones. By the early 1900's amateur and professional photographers began to create photographs that were printed on postcard stock using a special printing process. These had space on the back for the address, correspondence and stamp blocks for easy postage. The production of 'real' photographic postcards was made popular and easy by the development of the light handheld camera, the 'Kodak' introduced in 1903, which could be preloaded with roll film. Photographic postcards were produced in the millions during the war years by photographers who made a living by charging a shilling for half a dozen. These were less expensive than the traditional CDV and Cabinet Card and could be easily produced in large numbers in a format that enabled the soldier to easily post them home. It was common practice for an individual or unit to have a photograph taken upon completion of training, but it was the First World War 1914-1918 that gave rise to a huge popularity in photographs. On the continent local photographers quickly set up portable studios, often on a street or by a shell-damaged building, for soldiers to have their photographs taken. These field studios sprung up wherever the British soldier was stationed, from Alexandria and Cairo in Egypt, to Arras and Poperinghe in France and Flanders.

British Army 1900-1918

The period from the end of the Anglo-Boer War conflict in South Africa and the mobilization of the British Expeditionary Force (BEF) in 1914 was a time of great change for the British Army. In essence it was a time of reorganization, and formalization, to meet a perceived threat from Germany, and to ensure that the army could be easily expanded, reinforced and equipped in the event of a major European war. The Haldane Army Reforms of 1908 brought about the creation of the BEF, and established the Territorial Force (old Volunteer Force) to supplement the Regular Army and Special Reserve (old militia) units. These reforms were not only isolated to the British army's structure, but also to its uniforms and equipment.

On the eve of war in August 1914, the strength of the Regular British Army was about 235,000 men of whom 100,000 were already overseas on duties in India and the colonies. Additionally, there was the Reserve that numbered some 210,000, and the Terri-

Military Photographers R. Hughes and Sons, located near an army camp in Britain.

"English Spoken" A British GS Wagon in front of E. Voisin's photographic studio, named 'Photo Franco-Anglaise'. It was in this type of studio that many of the active service *Carte Postale's* were taken.

torial Force of about 251,000. When the BEF went to war, it was the only professional army in the world, and was also claimed to be 'the best trained, best organized and best equipped British Army that ever went forth to war'. The BEF comprised of six infantry divisions and a cavalry division, which by the spring of 1915 had expanded to eleven regular divisions in the field. Mobilization continued with battalions stationed abroad brought home whilst recruitment continued throughout the country. The Dominion's of Canada, Australia, New Zealand and South Africa also set about raising their own expeditionary forces in support of the Empire.

In Britain, Lord Kitchener, Secretary of State for War, recognized the need to support this force and immediately issued a 'Call to Arms', in which he asked for his first 100,000 men, under the famous slogan, 'Your Country Needs You'. A New Army, which became known as 'Kitchener's Army', was raised, and by the end of 1914 over a million men had volunteered. The ever-increasing demand for men saw the appointment of Lord Derby as the Director General of Recruiting. Lord Derby introduced conscription in 1916, initially for unmarried men, but soon it was necessary to call all men for service between the ages of eighteen and fifty-one. It had grown to over seventy infantry divisions in the field, including some ten Commonwealth divisions; five Australian, four Canadian and one New Zealand. In November 1918 the British Army numbered some three million officers and men, both frontline troops, and those performing a multitude of tasks from supplying food and ammunition to casualty care and evacuation.

General Uniform Description

The traditional mark of the British soldier for well over 200 years was his red coat, with bright white helmet and piped clay equipment, with shining brass buckles and badges. The uniform was eventually replaced in the field with lightweight sandy colored cotton called 'khaki', a Persian and Urdu word meaning dusty. This helped camouflage the soldier, enabling him to blend in with any sandy or rocky landscape. Although certain units from as early as the 1840's wore khaki, the dyes used were of poor quality, and it was not until 1884 when a permanent mineral khaki dye was patented. Troops on active service in Egypt, India and parts of Africa were allowed a Khaki Drill (KD) uniform, and in 1896 it was officially introduced for wear at all stations abroad. Soldiers still wore their whitened equipment and polished metal buckles and badges to serious consequences. During one of the early engagements during the Anglo-Boer War (1899-1902) a correspondent writing for the London *Daily Mail* wrote: "*Those gleaming insignia, the stars and buttons and buckles of the professional soldier, were all very well in the drawing-room. In the sunshine of the veldt they blazed like a heliograph. Against an invisible enemy, the British officers had been as conspicuous as redcoats*". The problem was not just isolated to officers as other ranks stood out just as much. Equipment was dyed a similar color, with the help of mud, tea, tobacco and even cow-dung, to that of the uniform and the brasses dulled in order to make the soldier less conspicuous. The wearing of KD in South Africa was soon found not to offer sufficient protection against the elements, so this gave rise to the introduction of a serge uniform (twilled worsted fabric) officially patent sealed in April 1900.

By the close of the Anglo-Boer War the British Army wore a mix of khaki drill and serge uniform in a range of styles, along with a wide variety of headgear and equipment, that overall gave little uniformity in army dress. A change was needed, thus in 1902 a universal pattern of drab (an earth brown color that was officially known as 'drab' but commonly called 'khaki') serge uniform was introduced for wear both at home and abroad. This had been successfully trialed during the Boer War with a patent being officially sealed in January 1902 (Army Orders 10 and 40). This uniform, designed so it would be suitable for all climates, according to how much, or how little, clothing was worn beneath it, became the standard Service Dress during the First World War (1914-1918).

Jackets and Trousers

By the start of the First World War the Victorian Full Dress uniform of scarlet, blue or green was virtually obsolete. A special Army Order declared that Service Dress was to be worn by all ranks for all purposes, except for ceremonial guard. The Pattern 1902 Service Dress jacket was described as being a loosely-fitting garment with a turned down 'rolled' collar, rifle patches on the shoulders, patch pockets on the breast, side pockets let into the skirts below the waist and with plain, removable shoulder straps. The shoulder straps were edged with a color to match the branch of service, e.g. scarlet for infantry, yellow for cavalry. Additional regimental distinctions were shown by strips of colored cloth on which were embroidered the units titles and worn on the upper arms. The issued buttons were the General Service (GS) pattern showing the Royal Coat of Arms for all regiments except Rifle regiments who wore black, or blackened, buttons.

The jacket went through several minor changes: in 1904 the removable shoulder straps were replaced with permanently attached straps made of twisted drab cord. By the end of that year the cord shoulder strap was replaced with sewn down cloth straps. In 1908 the embroidered titles were removed, and metal regimental titles were worn on the shoulder straps. This was the standard pattern worn by the opening months of the war. The major difference to this pattern was the doublet cut, issued to the Scottish kilted regiments that had the front skirts tailored back in order to provide space for the sporran. At this time there was no official change to the manufacturing process of the doublet style jacket, so it was left to the regimental tailor to modify them. The practice continued throughout the war, even after Army Orders (AO 356 and 391) in 1915 ordered this alteration to be stopped, due to the fact that rounding the skirts in wartime was unnecessary as sporrans were no longer worn in the field.

With the rapid progression of the war in late 1914, and Lord Kitchener's call for volunteers to take the 'Kings Shilling', an increasing demand was placed upon the army administration. This resulted in difficulties providing housing, clothing, equipment and training. Production of uniforms and equipment for the Regular, Reservists and Territorials, and now the newly raised 'Kitchener' battalions of the New Army, had the manufacturing industry working flat out. It was common to see the New Armies in training wearing an incongruous mixture of civilian and military garb. Due to shortages of the official drab serge uniform, an 'Emergency Pattern' dark blue serge uniform, commonly called the 'Kitchener blue' was made available. This was not popular with new recruits as it resembled too much the familiar civilian uniform of postmen, policemen and tram-drivers, and not that of a soldier. In order to increase production and easily bring on new clothing contractors with minimum effort, home and abroad, the service dress pattern was altered slightly in an effort to simplify its manufacture. This led to the introduction of the 'Simplified Jacket', which were produced in huge quantities throughout 1915. In general this jacket conformed to the description of the 1902 version, but had certain design details which were simplified or eliminated altogether. The most noticeable part of the change was the enlargement of the chest pockets with the pleats taken out, and the elimination of the rifle patches. When production caught up in late 1915 a reversion was made back to the standard 1902 pattern.

Rank insignia was worn on the arms in the traditional manner, as were badges of trade, proficiency and good conduct. The badges were either metal or drab worsted embroidery. Medal ribbons were also permitted to be worn on the jackets. Common worsted chevron stripes were worn on the arms as badges of rank, e.g. one chevron for a Lance Corporal, two for a Corporal and three for a Sergeant. The Trade Badges worn were either as appointment badges, e.g. bugler, scout, drummer, gun layer, or as skill-at-arms badges, e.g. marksman, machine gunner, bomber or as general trade badges, e.g. saddler, medical orderly, pioneer. These badges soon became supplemented by a new form of battle heraldry in the form of colored cloth signs, or 'battle patches' that blazoned everything from jackets and helmets, to vehicles and signposts. The battle patch was designed to identify a unit in a way that was not obvious to the enemy.

The Pattern 1902 SD trousers were universally worn by all arms of the service except the kilted regiments, Cavalry and other mounted services e.g. drivers, army cyclists and the Royal Flying Corps. For these units the trousers were tailored in a breech style 'pantaloon' and commonly made of Bedford cord material, more often than not reinforced at the inner thigh/knee for riding. Occasionally in the field trousers were cut-down into shorts, done either to combat the heat of the summer, or to lessen infection from lice. This became common practice not only in the Middle East, but also during the summer months on the Western Front before it was discouraged and finally prohibited by a General Routine Order (GRO 1850/1916) in October 1916. However by mid-1917 a pattern of shorts or knickerbockers were eventually approved for service dress issue. Khaki drill shorts and button-up Indian pattern 'Bombay Bloomers' were widely worn with the KD frock, little changed from the Victorian days, in the tropical climates of India and during the Middle-Eastern campaigns in Gallipoli, Mesopotamia and Palestine. Scottish soldiers who wore a tartan kilt in the field had this protected by a wrap-around khaki cloth cover or apron, worn with a diced hose, garters, khaki spats and highland shoes. By December 1914 shoes quickly gave way to the standard B-pattern field ankle-boot and puttees (the name 'puttee' coming from the Hindustani for bandages), as shoes proved not practical, especially in the glutinous mud of France and Flanders.

The regulations of 1902 also aimed to produce a universal field uniform for the officer. The officer's jacket was made up from 'special mixture serge' cloth of the same color as that of the other ranks, but of far better quality. This uniform was not issued, but purchased from authorized tailors, hatters and boot-makers at the officers' own expense. The pattern of jacket was loose fitting, but tailored at the waist with patch pockets on the breast and bellow pockets on the skirts below the waistband. A stand and fall collar fastened around the neck, whilst detachable shoulder straps had colored edging to match the branch of service, similar to the other ranks. The shoulder straps were replaced in 1904 with straps of twisted drab cord, and in 1913 these were replaced with sewn down, plain cloth shoulder straps. Rank insignia was initially worn on the cuffs using braided 'Austrian knots', that was replaced early in 1902 (AO 261/1902) with a vertical crows' feet cuff rank design. Guards and Cavalry regiments did not wear cuff braid, but chose instead to wear their rank on their shoulder straps. Bronze collars, cap badges and buttons were worn to reflect the Regiment or Corps the officer belonged to. In 1913 (AO 279/1913) the closed stand and fall collar was replaced with an open, step collar to reveal the shirt and tie, thereby reducing the five large buttons down the front to four. Trousers were made in a similar material to the jacket, and were worn with shoes. 'Knickerbocker' style breeches were common wear in the field and worn with brown leather ankle boots and drab puttees. Bedford cord material breeches were commonly worn by mounted officers, with cloth puttees or brown leather 'Stohwasser' leggings fastened with a spiral strap, field-boots and spurs. During the early part of the war the popular, but conspicuous light-colored caps, ties, collars, shirts and breeches were soon discarded for articles of the more regulation darker drab.

Due to the high casualty rate of officers during the early part of the First World War, changes to their dress were soon introduced. By late 1915 some officers started to move their rank insignia from the cuff to the shoulder and by 1916 jackets were manufactured in an authorized shoulder rank pattern. These became known as 'Wind-up' jackets. Wind-up was an expression of contempt by officers, and some believed that minimizing the visibility of an officer, by any means, was a sign of cowardice, hence "he's got the wind-up". In battle, when going over the top, infantry officers soon adopted, by order, the other ranks SD jacket, often referred to as a 'Tommy' jacket, after Tommy Atkins the popular slang term for a British soldier. This was yet another method of making the officer less conspicuous to the enemy marksman. Both the Wind-up and the Tommy jackets were unpopular with most officers, so the cuff rank style continued to be worn throughout the war.

Headgear

To partner the new Service Dress a universal form of headgear, called the 'Brodrick' cap, was introduced in 1903. This forage cap proved very unpopular and only worn briefly, with or without a khaki cover, until it was replaced in 1905. Prior to that date a variety of headgear was worn. Most common was the Field Service 'fore and aft' sidecap, officially called 'cap, forage' which dated back to the 1890's. This cap had a band that could be let down to form a type of balaclava, fastening with two small buttons under the chin. It became popular with the Royal Flying Corps, who chose to adopt it as part of their service dress in 1912. Also quite common was the wide brimmed felt slouch hat, sometimes referred to as a 'Smasher', which became widely worn during the Boer War, and issued again to the British for the Salonika campaign. For wear in more temperate climates overseas the 1870's style of Foreign Service helmet was worn, until it was replaced in 1903 by the 'Wolseley' Pattern sun helmet. Scottish regiments wore their own distinctive variety of headgear. In 1914 the dark blue 'Glengarry' with its small pom-pom or tourie in the middle of the crown and regimental diced band was worn. A 'Balmoral' bonnet was also issued in dark-blue that was sometimes worn with a khaki cover, which was replaced by the spring of 1915 with a purpose made drab colored bonnet. In 1916 the 'Tam-o'-shanter', a larger and floppier version of the Balmoral bonnet, was issued and became the universal Scottish headdress for the remainder of the war.

The Pattern 1905 SD cap, introduced as a replacement for the unpopular Brodrick cap, was made of the same drab serge material as the jacket and trousers, and was worn by all arms of the service. Officers wore a tailored version of this cap that was introduced slightly earlier in 1902 with the officer's service dress. The first change to the SD cap was during the winter of 1914/15 when a soft winter cap was issued in December 1914 (General Routine Order 377/1914). This was nicknamed the 'Gor'blimey', reputedly by the first Sergeant-Major to set eyes on one. The style was also used in officers' hats at the time, although tailored to give them a much smarter appearance. The 1905 SD cap soon obtained a common floppy style that was achieved by removing the wire stiffeners (GRO 902/1915), and by the autumn of 1916 the SD cap was replaced altogether with an official soft, floppy version. This new cap, first issued in spring 1916 (RACD 8706/1916), was referred to as the 'Soft cap' and became very popular, so much so that by 1917 the 1905 SD cap and Gor'blimey had almost ceased to be worn.

During the latter stages of 1915 the steel 'shrapnel' helmet designed by Brodie, nicknamed the 'battle-bowler' or just plain 'tin-hat', began to be issued to the men in the frontlines. Initially the steel helmets were on short supply, but by the 1916 Somme battles the helmet was on general issue (GRO 1602/1916). To help prevent light reflection helmets were issued with covers, made of hessian sacking or khaki drill cloth. If these were not available mud made an effective alternative, until helmets were produced with a dulled rough sandy finish.

Protective Clothing

With the Pattern 1902 uniform a greatcoat made of a "drab mixture of milled and waterproofed cloth" was also authorized for issue. The other ranks greatcoat came in two versions, a dismounted and a mounted style. The dismounted pattern was a long single breasted garment, similar to the Victorian blue-grey greatcoat worn during the Boer War. It had rifle patches and a small ticket pocket, with two further pockets at the waist and turned back cuffs. As with the SD jacket in 1915, to simplify manufacture, the greatcoat was soon made without the rifle patches, ticket pocket and towards the end of the war the turned back cuffs were also eliminated. Mounted troops wore the mounted pattern distinguished by its double-breasted front and shorter knee-length cut. Officers also wore a greatcoat that was a long double-breasted garment with turned back cuffs, and shoulder straps that displayed badges of rank. A semi-official shorter cut double-breasted coat with leather football buttons, referred to as the 'British Warm', became popular, and was similar in design to the mounted other ranks greatcoat. Also immensely popular with officers was a wide variety of privately purchased raincoats, known as 'Trench Coats', famously the 'Burberry' and 'Macintosh', that still remain popular today.

As the misery of life in open trenches began to be experienced, protective clothing was issued to the BEF in the hope of keeping down the numbers of men going sick with trench foot, frostbite and exposure. Soldiers in the trenches and those employed in exposed roles, e.g. drivers, dispatch riders and sentries, were issued with a variety of waterproof clothing. This ranged from waterproofed Sou'wester style jackets and trouser leggings to oil-dressed and indiarubber waterproof coats and capes. Most of the infantry however had to make do with their issue rectangular groundsheet to keep off the rain until a purpose designed waterproofed indiarubber cape was officially issued in 1917. Animal fur coats, commonly made from goat or sheepskin, and leather jerkins were issued during the winters, whilst rubber gum boot waders helped the feet to stay dry. Waterproof covers were issued for the SD cap, the Gor'blimey and the Scottish bonnets, whilst in hot weather neck curtains were authorized to help protect the neck from the sun. Woolen cap comforters were popular with the troops, and a multitude of privately purchased and home knitted gifts were provided. Everything from scarves, gloves and socks to various designs of balaclava helmet were sent to the men in the trenches, all offering added protection and comfort from the extremes of the weather.

General Infantry Equipment Description

At the dawn of the 20th Century, the white pipe-clayed leather Pattern 1888 Valise Equipment of the 'Slade Wallace' design was still being worn, although a replacement was already being looked for. In 1903 the official commission into the Boer War harshly criticized the valise equipment, acting on complaints about lost ammunition from the pouches as well as the equipment being badly balanced, heavy and generally very cumbersome. Swift reforms were needed, which led to the immediate manufacture and issue in late 1903 of "Bandolier Equipment, Pattern 1903". This consisted of a brown leather waist belt, leather charger-loaded cartridge belt pouches, leather frog for the Pattern 1903 bayonet, canvas haversack, water-bottle holder, mess-tin with cover, a webbing greatcoat carrier and a 50-round leather bandolier. The bandolier was issued for all services, worn over the left shoulder it had five ten-round cartridge pockets on the front. There was also a 90-round version of the bandolier that had four extra pockets on the back, and worn by mounted services. Even with the introduction of the Pattern 1903, the obsolete Slade Wallace was still worn, albeit with the Full Dress uniform. The British Army continued to seek better designed equipment, and soon the Pattern 1903 was superceded with the 'Mills' Pattern 1908 Web Equipment, as initially manufactured by the Mills Equipment Company, and accepted into service in 1908.

The Mills equipment was made of woven cotton webbing and assembled as one piece so it could be put on or taken off very quickly. The equipment was probably one of the most comfortable and functional sets of infantry equipment used by any army at that time. The Pattern 1903 equipment could only carry 100 rounds of ammunition, but the Mills could carry 150 rounds, the recognized minimum at the time. "Web Equipment, Pattern 1908", as it was officially called, became the standard infantry equipment worn by the British and their Commonwealth and Dominion troops during the First World War. The basic set consisted of a wide webbing waist belt with two angled buckles at the rear, to which the shoulder straps were attached. The straps went over the shoulder and buckled to the left and right hand ammunition pouches at the front of the belt. The left and right hand ammunition pouches consisted of five individual pockets, three underneath and two above, each containing fifteen rounds. When the 'ammo' pouches were not worn, the shoulder straps could be attached to a pair of brace attachments, or simply looped about the belt. An entrenching tool head carrier and water bottle carrier were also worn at or below the waist. The entrenching tool was a two-piece device, the handle of which was carried strapped to the bayonet scabbard, and attached to the bayonet frog, which would carry the Pattern 1907 sword bayonet. A haversack was supplied that officially contained iron rations (1 lb. of biscuits, 1 tin of 'bully beef', 2-oz. sugar and 1/2 oz. tea), knife, fork and spoon, tin of oil and a flannel 'four by two' for cleaning the rifle. The standard infantry D-shaped mess tin with cover could be carried, attached to the haversack or large pack. The large pack officially contained the greatcoat, hold-all (containing shaving kit, comb, tooth brush, spare laces and soap), 'housewife', towel, brushes, cardigan (winter only), cap comforter, change of underclothing, including shirt and socks and a groundsheet which was folded under the flap. The entire equipment, including rifle and ammunition, weighed about 60-lbs. This, of course, did not include any other accoutrements of war, e.g. wire-cutters, gas helmets, emergency bandoliers or grenades.

When war broke out the equipment suppliers, similar to the clothing industry, were soon struggling to cope with the high production demands that were placed upon them. This gave rise not only to the reissuing of the Pattern 1903 equipment as a stopgap, but also the issuing of older stocks of the Slade Wallace Valise Equipment, although admittedly for training purposes only. The supply problem became so bad that a new leather set of equipment was manufactured called "Infantry Equipment, Pattern 1914". The pattern for this equipment was sealed on August 30th, 1914, and consisted of a leather belt with snake buckle, a pair of brace straps, leather carriers for a water bottle, an entrenching tool handle and head and a bayonet, which went together with a pair of 60 round ammunition pouches. Additionally there was a webbing large pack and a small haversack carried, similar to the Pattern 1908. The equipment was made of pliable leather and colored in what was called 'London brown'. The New Kitchener Armies were amongst the first to receive the Pattern 1914, although the preference was certainly for the lighter 'Regular Army' webbing. When stocks of 1908 and 1914 equipment were sufficient by early 1916, the 1903 equipment was generally replaced. However it was not until the latter stages of the war when sufficient quantities of the Pattern 1908 were available, that the Pattern 1914 was eventually withdrawn.

At the turn of the 20th Century field officers' standard equipment consisted of the Sam Browne belt. The 'Sam Browne' (invented by General Sir Sam Browne VC) dated back to the 1860's, and had changed little in design, worn throughout the Boer War and the First World War, it is still in use by many of today's armies. Initially worn for Foreign Service, it was only approved for Home Service in 1899. It was originally designed to carry only the officers' sword, pistol holster and ammunition pouch, but soon carried a wide array of supplementary accoutrements that could be worn either on a belt loop (e.g. binoculars and compass), or on short snap hook straps (e.g. haversack, map case, water bottle). In the frontline, the practicalities of trench warfare saw the Sam Browne fall quickly into disuse with preference for the standard infantry equipment. In January 1915 an Army Order (GRO 429/1914) was published that stated that officers in the line were to wear the same equipment as the men. This helped the officer, without his telltale trappings, to be less conspicuous in the field to the enemies' marksmen. This order was often ignored and the Sam Browne continued to be worn, in and out of the line, as was various styles of commercial equipment. Available to officers from various outfitters, these ranged in many different styles and manufactured in leather, canvas and webbing materials. There was even a webbing officer set produced by Mills in 1917 that resembled the World War II Pattern 1937 Webbing Equipment.

Dominion Troops

Canadian Expeditionary Force

The Canadian Expeditionary Force (CEF) had their own pattern of service dress uniform, the Pattern 1903, which was loosely based on the Pattern 1902 SD as worn by the British. The main difference was that the Canadian jacket had seven front buttons instead of five, pointed cuffs and a stand collar. Early versions of the 1903 jacket had colored shoulder straps to denote the service, e.g. yellow for cavalry, red for artillery, blue for infantry. In late 1914 the pattern was modified with plain shoulder straps, although soldiers from the First Canadian Contingent were still wearing colored shoulders when they arrived on the Western Front in 1915. By 1917 the standard British 1902 SD jacket had become officially approved by Canada and replaced the 1903 SD jacket when stocks became depleted. The Canadians wore the same headdress as the British, although some support units had their own variety of the Gor'blimey cap, distinguishable by a small button to the front that secured fold-down earflaps.

As the CEF was just as short of equipment during the early part of the war as the British, they brought to England a variety of their own Militia equipment. This included the brown leather 'Oliver' valise pattern, which had been in use by the Canadians since the 1890's, and the webbing 'Mills Burrowes' Pattern 1913 equipment. Most of the new battalions of the CEF were issued Pattern 1908, but this still left some of the Regular Army and the newly formed Princess Patricia's Canadian Light Infantry wearing the Mills Burrowes equipment, until British stores could supply them with Pattern 1908. The Mills Burrowes was slightly different to the standard Pattern 1908, characteristic in photographs by its narrow braces, cartridge pouch design, belt clasp and entrenching tool carrier on the water bottle. In May 1915 it was decided to improve the Oliver equipment by making a few design alterations. This would be known as the Pattern 1915 which was issued to the Second Canadian Division and used in training but was not taken to France. In late 1915 the Oliver equipment was again re-designed and became known as the Pattern 1916. This pattern was mainly used in training, but also saw some service in France by the Fourth Canadian Division.

Australian and New Zealand Army Corps (ANZAC)

The Australian soldier wore his own distinctive pattern of SD jacket, officially called 'Jackets, S.D. Australian'. This woolen drab serge jacket was loose fitting, with button up cuffs and baggy bellow hip pockets. The rising sun badge, as adopted in 1904, of the Australian Imperial Force (AIF) was commonly worn as collar dogs, with metal 'AUSTRALIA' shoulder titles. Due to supply shortages later in the war, it was not uncommon to see Australians in issued British SD, but this was unpopular and as soon as sufficient supplies of the Australian SD were available, the jackets were replaced.

With the jacket pantaloon cord breeches were worn together with the popular slouch hat, officially known as 'Hat, Khaki fur felt', adopted by Australia in the 1890's. It was made of either a fur felt (rabbit's fur) or wool felt, and was worn with a puggaree (from the Indian word 'Pagri'), either a muslin cloth folded about the crown of the hat or just a simple woolen band. The hat could be worn with the left side of the brim laying flat or the brim could be held to the side of the hat by a press stud or a small flat hook and square loop. The Australian rising sun hat badge was worn on the upturned left side of the hat, although men of the Australian Third Division wore their slouch hats with the left side turned down and badge to the front, an order from their commanding officer in an effort to instill an *esprit de corps*. At the start of the war the AIF were issued a peaked SD cap, similar to that worn by the British, but distinguishable by a leather-trimmed peak. These were mainly worn by the Australian First Division, and commonly seen in photographs in training camps in Australia and Egypt, as well as in the trenches at Gallipoli. By the time the Australians had reached the Western Front the slouch hat had become common wear, and an Australian trademark.

Australia adopted the Pattern 1908 equipment shortly after the British. At the beginning of the war it was found that the overseas supply and production of the web equipment could not be relied upon so the Australian Government sent out local contracts for the production of a trial leather version, based upon the Pattern 1908, and referred to as the Pattern 1908/15 equipment. This was a copy of the web equipment, although early attempts varied in the type of ammunition pouch closures and securing methods. Some of this equipment found its way to the battlefields although most was worn in the training camps in Australia, Egypt and England. In 1916 a report into the Australian leather equipment condemned it when compared with the webbing version. The major complaint was the equipment stretched and slipped when wet. This problem was attended to by adding tongues to the buckles, but despite these modifications the leather equipment does not seem to have enjoyed much popularity after 1916, and was quickly replaced with the Pattern 1908.

The New Zealand soldier wore a pattern of SD jacket manufactured in New Zealand that was almost identical, apart from some minor differences in pocket and rifle pad detail, to the British 1902 SD. In 1915 most of the New Zealanders wore either the British 1905 SD cap or the Australian style slouch hat with the exception of the artillery, Otago Mounted Rifles and the Wellington Infantry. These units had a similar fur hat, but wore it with the brim down and the crown creased with four dents, into a 'lemon-squeezer' shape. Each branch of service wore a different color puggaree on the hat; khaki/red for infantry, khaki/blue for sappers, khaki/maroon for Field Ambulance etc. This hat, as instituted by Lt. Col. William Malone, the commander of the Wellington Infantry Battalion, soon became a trademark of the New Zealand soldier. By the time the New Zealanders had left Gallipoli for the Western Front, virtually all wore this pattern of 'Kiwi' hat, enforced by Major General Godley in an effort to standardize headdress. Apart from this, the New Zealanders were basically clothed and equipped the same as the British.

Royal Flying Corps

The Royal Flying Corps (RFC) was a corps of the British Army, founded from the Air Battalion of the Royal Engineers in 1912. The army's RFC and the navy's Royal Naval Air Service (RNAS) were combined to form the world's largest, and the first independent air service, the Royal Air Force (RAF) on April 1st, 1918.

RFC officers wore either the universal service dress peaked cap as introduced in 1902 or the Field Service forage cap as introduced in 1913. With this the Pattern 1912 jacket, as officially introduced in November 1913, was worn. This became known as the 'Maternity' jacket because it was said to resemble clothing worn by expectant mothers. The jacket was normal length but cut with an extended flap, initially falling vertically at the swell of the collarbone, and later at the point of the shoulder, which fastened with concealed horn buttons down the right side of the body. It had the typical stand and fall collar of the time, shoulder straps with rank and plain cuffs with a tab that could be press-studded tighter when wearing flying gauntlets. Sam Browne equipment was worn, along with breeches or straight leg trousers, and un-studded shoes or ankle boots. Soon the maternity gave way to the standard Pattern 1913 Officer's SD that was worn with bronzed RFC collar dogs and brass RFC buttons. RNAS officers initially wore a distinctive naval dark blue doubled breasted jacket, often called a 'Monkey Jacket' with a gold eagle and rank lace on the cuffs. When serving overseas they quickly adopted the single breasted army style of uniform, officially adopted in November 1916, but worn with naval cuff rank. It is interesting to note that during the war officers who were seconded into squadrons, continued to wear their own regimental service dress and insignia, until they were officially gazetted.

With the creation of the RAF a new uniform was introduced by Air Force Memorandum No.2 (AFM 2). Two uniforms were initially laid down for officers, both exactly the same cut; however they were in two different colors; khaki and pale blue-grey. The jacket had no shoulder straps, four gilt RAF single-breasted buttons, with two breast patch pockets and two large bellow hip pockets and a fabric waist belt with a single-pronged gilt buckle. Rank was worn on the cuffs as well as on the peaked cap. The peaked cap was similar in style to the Pattern 1905, but had a black patent leather peak and chin strap with a black mohair band to which was applied the new RAF badge. Gilt rank bars were originally worn on the cap, either side of the RAF badge, but in July 1918 they were eradicated. The new uniform saw service during the latter half of 1918, but was slow to be universally worn as the 'wearing out' period of the earlier uniforms seemed to have lasted through to the end of the war.

Other ranks also wore the Pattern 1912 'Maternity' jacket, but made of a drab serge material with cloth 'ROYAL FLYING CORPS' insignia worn on the arms, along with badges of rank or trade. Pantaloon style breeches were worn with infantry puttees and boots. The 'Maternity' went through several changes after its introduction; extending the flap to close at the point of the shoulders, adding of shoulder straps, button closing flapped horizontal pockets instead of vertical ones, and the elimination of the cuff tightening tabs. Headgear worn was initially the 1905 SD cap but was soon replaced with the Field Service forage cap. A 'maternity' style Pattern 1913 knee-length greatcoat, in similar cut to the officer's greatcoat, was worn in cold weather. The army's Pattern 1902 uniform was commonly worn from 1917 onwards, especially when RFC clothing stocks were purposely run low to coincide with the creation of the RAF. It was not until late 1918 that the new 'blue' other ranks RAF uniform was sanctioned.

The aviator's leather flying coats came commonly in two styles, a short and long pattern. Most were in brown leather, but some others were in black, especially those worn by the RNAS. The RNAS, in May 1915, even introduced a special pattern blue overcoat with belt to be worn as flying kit, but these were rarely worn for this purpose. The RFC's short pattern flying jacket, which had a camel fleece lining, was introduced in 1912, and improved with a later pattern in September 1913. This was mid-thigh length with a crossover piece that contained an angled chest map pocket. It also had large flapped pockets on the front skirt of the coat. Leather trousers were issued with this coat that had a distinctive front flap opening. A longer flying coat was introduced late in 1915 that was similar in style to the short pattern with its large chest map pocket. As for the infantry officer, retailers like Burberrys and Gamages advertised several different designs of privately purchased flying garments to "safeguard the airman". These included models like the Burberry 'Tielocken' and the 'Air-Warm' made in proofed Burberry material and lined with thick camel fleece. A privately designed non-leather flying suit was eventually adopted by the War Office as a sealed pattern in December 1917, called the 'Sidcot'. This consisted of an outer layer of proofed khaki twill over a rubberized muslin inter-lining with a mohair liner. This also had a chest map pocket as well as knee pockets. This became the classic late war flying suit as leather garments were phased out by the Air Ministry.

Two common patterns of flying boots were the 'Boots, Knee', as first introduced in October 1914 and later a thigh-length sheepskin boot, officially sealed as 'Boots, Thigh' in December 1916. The latter were designed by Major Hawker VC, DSO, and were popularly known as the 'Fug Boot'. Leather and fur backed gauntlets were very popular, especially the fingered glove that also had an attached mitten stitched to the back of the hand. An early pattern flying helmet used by the RFC was the tall domed brown 'Warren' helmet officially introduced in August 1914, and the French made 'Roold' helmet that was commonly used in France during the early days of the war. Most observers wore the soft leather balaclava helmet, known as a 'Cowl' helmet, whilst pilots typically wore a cap-type helmet similar to motoring caps of the time, both officially sealed patterns and privately purchased. There were also many variations of flying goggles, mainly made commercially with Triplex Safety Glass. An early issued goggle was made of a red rubber frame with an elastic strap, but by the autumn of 1915 these were relegated to transport drivers and dispatch riders. It wasn't until 1916 that an official pattern of flying goggle was introduced, called 'Goggle Mask, Mk I', soon to be improved by a Mark II version in 1917. As photographs show, much of the flying clothing during this period was privately purchased which led to little uniformity within the service. Uniformity was also lacking in the general service dress of the RAF, and even by November 1918 there was still a wide variety of dress being worn, evident in photographs of the period.

The Photographs

Chapter One

1900-1914

A fine Victorian studio portrait of a sergeant in 'Full Service Marching Order' (FSMO), c. 1901. He wears a Pattern 1900 serge uniform with buff leather Pattern 1888 Valise Equipment, and is armed with a Lee-Metford 303-inch rifle. Note the compass pouch on his belt.

A studio photograph of Imperial Yeomanry (IY) trooper's c.1900. They wear the IY style serge jacket, slouch hat with puggaree, mounted pattern Bedford cord breeches, puttees and ankle boots with spurs. Both wear the 100-round Mills and Orndorff Pattern webbing bandolier and are armed with 'long' Lee-Enfield 303-inch rifles.

An unidentified soldier is wearing the Pattern 1900 serge uniform with a felt slouch hat, buff leather belt, Pattern 1888 bayonet and a 100-round Mills and Orndorff webbing bandolier. He is armed with a 'long' Lee-Enfield.

A trooper from the Royal Dragoons in the Pattern 1896 khaki drill (KD) uniform. Note the slouch hat with silk scarf. Armed with a 'long' Lee-Metford rifle with mounted configuration sling, the ammunition is carried in a Pattern 1884 50-round web bandolier with leather flaps.

Above: A Trooper from the 11th (Yorkshire Dragoons) Company, Imperial Yeomanry c.1901. He wears a serge uniform, slouch hat, 100-round Mills and Orndorff bandolier, Bedford cord breeches, leather leggings and ankle boots with spurs.

Above right: A variation of an IY serge jacket with horn buttons. He also wears the typical slouch hat with puggaree and webbing bandolier. The Mills and Orndorff bandolier saw wide use during the Boer War, and manufactured in 50, 60, 70, 80 and 100 round versions, with and without flap covers.

Right: Trooper J.P. Collier, 27th (Devon) Company, Imperial Yeomanry. He wears the IY style serge jacket, a slouch hat and a Mills and Orndorff bandolier. Collier was taken prisoner during the Boer War, captured at Nooitgedacht in South Africa on December 13th, 1900.

Above: Private Charles Walter Forrest, Army Ordnance Corps. He wears a Pattern 1896 KD uniform, slouch hat and the 60-round Pattern 1901 leather bandolier. Notice the long service and good conduct chevron for two years service. The Pattern 1901 bandolier, manufactured for use by cavalry and mounted infantry, superseded the Pattern 1882, until this too was superseded by the Pattern 1903.

Above left: A New Zealand trooper, wearing a KD jacket with typical slouch hat and Mills and Orndorff webbing bandolier. He wears the 'NZ' fern leaf collar badges.

Left: A proudly posed Imperial Yeomanry sergeant wearing the Boer War 'Queens South Africa' and 'Kings South Africa' campaign medals. He wears an IY pattern of jacket with the leather Pattern 1882 'Bandolier, Mounted Infantry, Mark I'.

As the Boer War turned into a Guerrilla war, the British soldier soon adapted his dress to a lighter 'Commando' style. This photo shows an infantryman in the Pattern 1900 serge uniform, slouch hat, 100-round Mills and Orndorff webbing bandolier and 'long' Lee-Enfield 303 rifle c.1902.

A formal cabinet photograph showing a very smartly dressed Imperial Yeomanry sergeant. He wears yet another style of the serge jacket with an S-buckle belt and the 50-round Pattern 1882 leather bandolier, officially called 'Bandolier, Mounted Infantry, Mark I'.

Victorian Lancashire Fusilier officer in a KD uniform with marching order double strap Sam Browne belt. He also wears leather 'Stohwasser' leggings and holds a Wolseley Pattern solar topee c.1900. This distinctive look made the officer an easier target for the Boer marksman.

Above: Victorian Infantry officer in a khaki serge uniform with leather 'football' buttons, double strap Sam Browne belt with sword and 'Stohwasser' leather leggings. He wears the typical forage cap of the time.

Opposite
Top:A draft for South Africa wearing the Pattern 1900 serge service dress uniform, and Pattern 1888 Valise Equipment with slouch hats.

Bottom: No.2 Section, 'E' Company, East Yorkshire Regiment photographed at Farnborough, Hampshire. They are wearing scarlet 7-button Full Dress (FD) jackets with white regimental cuff facings, dark-blue trousers with scarlet welt down the seam and forage caps. One soldier wears a scarlet 5-button undress frock.

E. Coy
No 2. SECTION.
East. Yorkshire Regt.

Above: Soldiers from the 3rd Volunteer Battalion, Hampshire Regiment wearing Full Dress, an 1880 pattern peaked forage cap and the later issue Brodrick caps c.1905. The scarlet FD jacket went into stores as soon as the Pattern 1902 SD jacket became universally available. By 1914 the jacket was virtually obsolete and used only for ceremonial guard.

Opposite
Top: The Irish Guards shooting team in Aldershot, 1903. All are wearing the Brodrick caps, first issued in 1903, with the first issue Pattern 1902 SD jacket with removable shoulder straps. The Brodrick was designed by William St.John Freemantle Brodrick, later Lord Midleton, Secretary of State for War.

Bottom: Royal Garrison Artillery gunners in a mix of Pattern 1902 SD jackets, with removable shoulder straps, and the modified 1904 variation that had twisted shoulder cords. 'RGA' embroidered cloth titles are worn, sewn to the top of each arm. Most are wearing Brodrick caps.

The unpopular Brodrick cap, officially called 'Cap, Forage, universal' is shown here being worn by two men of the Gloucestershire Regiment c.1905. They wear the early 'Slade Wallace' Valise Equipment with Pattern 1888 pouches.

A young private wearing the Pattern 1902 SD jacket with twisted shoulder cords, and a set of 'Slade Wallace' Valise Equipment. Note the Pattern 1882 pouches and the Oliver pattern of water bottle that dates back to the 1870's. The slouch hat, popularized during the Boer War, was worn at home as late as 1905 by some regiments.

"SLIDING ON THE PAVEMENT IS STRICTLY FORBIDDEN" An early photograph taken around 1908 shows the spiked blue cloth Pattern 1878 'Home Service' helmet, the 'Dress Service' and 'Service Dress' caps, the scarlet 'Full Dress' jacket and variations of the Pattern 1902 SD jacket.

Left: A lance corporal wearing the first issue of the Pattern 1902 SD jacket with removable shoulder straps. He also wears the Pattern 1882 leather bandolier, which was still in use by some troops up to and including the First World War.

Opposite
Top: A pre-war photograph of scouts from the 1/9th (Queen Victoria's Rifles) Battalion, London Regiment. They are individually equipped with binoculars and wear the *Fleur-de-Lys* scout badge on the right arm.

Bottom: Men from the 1/8th (Isle of Wight Rifles) Battalion, Hampshire Regiment, armed with 'long' Lee-Enfield's and wearing an obsolete pattern of volunteer brown leather Oliver Equipment. Due to shortages of equipment at the beginning of the war old stock was issued from stores, and in some cases purchased commercially by regiments. The photographed was taken at Sandown Barracks in 1915.

109

238

Above: A 'Kitchener blues' group, with 'long' Lee-Enfield rifles. They wear the emergency pattern 'blues' uniform that was not popular with the men as it resembled too much the familiar civilian uniform of postmen, policemen and tram-drivers.

Opposite
Top: A machinegun team from the 1/25th (Cyclist) Battalion, London Regiment in 1914. They wear the Pattern 1902 SD jacket with forage cap and the pattern of leather equipment unique to this unit. The wheel-mounted machine-gun is a commercially made 303-inch Model 1895 Colt-Browning.

Bottom: Recruits in their emergency pattern 'Kitchener blues' uniform, wearing obsolete Pattern 1888 Valise Equipment and armed with Lee-Metford 303-inch rifles.

283.

A Kitchener recruit from the 9th Battalion, East Surrey Regiment, photographed at Kingston-on-Thames, Surrey in September 1914. Note the "9 Est Surrey" cloth insignia worn on the arm in lieu of the regulation regimental badges.

A young Kitchener volunteer wearing an obsolete set of Victorian Valise Equipment with Pattern 1882 pouches. He is armed with a Short Magazine Lee Enfield (SMLE) and Pattern 1907 sword bayonet.

Opposite
A volunteer from the 10th (Grimsby) Battalion, Lincolnshire Regiment or 'Grimsby Pals' in early 1915. He appears to be wearing a Home Service Dress cap with his newly issued set of Pattern 1914 Infantry Equipment.

A soldier from the 5th Battalion, South Lancashire Regiment. He wears a commercial variation of the Pattern 1908 webbing equipment with three-pocket pouches instead of five. This pattern of equipment was purchased for some Territorial Regiments whilst training in England.

A young Leicestershire Territorial bugler wearing the County TF Association set of Pattern 1908 webbing equipment with three-pocket pouches and variation press studs on the ends of the shoulder braces. Note also the buglers metal trade badge.

Men from the 7th Battalion, King's (Liverpool Regiment) at Redbridge, September 1914. The sentry wears Pattern 1908 equipment with a pre-war trial pattern of water bottle, distinguished by the large funnel top.

Left: 1/7th (Cyclist) Battalion, Welsh Regiment volunteer wearing a 'Brethyn Llwyd', or Welsh grey 'homespun' uniform with black rifles buttons. This uniform was made by Welsh woolen mills in the Cardiff area at the start of the war and chosen in preference to the 'blues' uniform. The serge uniform was of a slightly more brown shade than 'regulation', and thus prompted the nickname 'The Chocolate Soldiers'. He holds an Arisaka carbine.

Opposite

Top: Cyclists from the 1/9th (Cyclist) Battalion Hampshire Regiment in England with a variety of equipment, including Pattern 1908 webbing in War Office and commercial varieties. Note the man on the left wears the 'T 9 Hants' shoulder title as a cap badge. This battalion saw service in India and in late 1918 was sent to Siberia as part of the Allied Intervention in Russia.

Bottom: Men from the 5th (Cyclist) Battalion, East Yorkshire Regiment, Xmas 1914. Note the Balaclavas and the large woolen hat on the sergeant. All are wearing volunteer pattern equipment that was superseded by Pattern 1908 or 1914 as war progressed.

"Yrieston Shore" (outpost) 5th (Cyclists) E.Y. Rgt Xmas 1914.

A Scottish soldier wearing a variation of the Pattern 1903 Bandolier Equipment that was issued to some of the Kitchener battalions. Note the style of shoulder braces that differs from the standard Pattern 1903.

A different view of the same equipment being worn showing details of the Pattern 1903 canvas haversack and mess-tin cover. The 'D' or kidney-section mess-tin was used by the British Army from the 1820s up until the Second World War.

A soldier from the Cheshire Regiment in camp wearing Pattern 1903 Bandolier Equipment. He is armed with the 303-inch charger loading Lee-Enfield Mk.I. Note the 15-round Mark II cartridge pockets, as introduced in 1906. These were designed to be outward opening to help prevent loss of ammunition.

"The Compliments of the Season" Three soldiers wearing Pattern 1903 bandoliers, belts and the early pattern canvas haversack. The rifles are 303-inch Lee-Metford's. Note the caps being worn with chinstraps.

Men of the Royal Warwickshire Regiment wearing full sets of Pattern 1903 Bandolier Equipment with 15-round Mark I cartridge pockets.

A soldier displays two front views of the Pattern 1908 Infantry Web Equipment. The only two companies, who had looms to produce the equipment, specifically the pouches, were the 'Mills Equipment Company' and 'M. Wright & Sons'.

MARCHING ORDER WITH WATERPROOF SHEET.

MARCHING ORDER WITH BLANKET.

Two views of the web Pattern 1908 Infantry Equipment in marching order with the large pack containing the rectangular groundsheet, and the issue blanket.

New recruits from the 1/10th (Scottish) Battalion, King's (Liverpool Regiment). Note the mix of service dress, and those in civilian clothes wearing tartan brassards, or armlets. The battalion wore the Forbes tartan kilt. The photograph is dated November 27th, 1914.

6th Battalion, Lincolnshire Regiment volunteers at Belton Park, September 1914. They wear a mix of the emergency 'Kitchener blues' uniform as well as newly issued service dress. The battalion sailed for Gallipoli in July 1915, and later saw service on the Western Front with the 11th (Northern) Division.

Recruits from the 28th (Artists Rifles) Battalion, London Regiment. This battalion became an Officers Training Corps based at Bailleul and later in St Omer, France. In late June 1917 the battalion joined the 63rd (Royal Naval) Division.

8th Battalion, Middlesex Regiment recruiting office. Amongst the wide array of recruiting posters shown here are "Remember the Lusitania" and "8th Middlesex Regiment Urgently Requires Reinforcements – Join At Once". RMS Lusitania was sunk off the Irish coast by submarine U-20 on May 7th 1915 with a loss of 1200 civilian lives. The disaster was instrumental in edging the United States closer into war, and served as a convenient propaganda tool to help bolster recruitment.

Chapter Two

Staff Officers and Others

A British major-general in a khaki covered dress cap, with red cap band, crossed sword-and-baton cap badge, gold oak-leaf peak lace and gorget patches. The shoulder rank of a crossed Mameluke saber and baton with a star above denotes the rank of a major-general.

A general, distinguishable by a red cap band, crossed sword-and-baton cap badge, two rows of gold oak-leaf peak lace, or 'scrambled egg' and gorget patches. Officers above the rank of colonel wore badges of rank on their shoulder straps, not their cuff.

Above: A Royal Engineer brigade staff colonel wearing a khaki covered cap, scarlet gorget patches with gold chain gimp lines and the Royal Crest staff cap badge. He wears ribbons for the Military Cross (MC) and the 1914 'Mons' Star. The photo is dated October 8th, 1919.

Above right: A Wiltshire Regiment Staff Captain, wearing a khaki cloth covered dress cap, and scarlet gorget patches with a central line of crimson silk gimp to both lapels, denoting a staff appointment.

Right: A staff captain in a Pattern 1913 chevron-laced cuff-rank jacket with red gorget insignia. He is wearing the blue undress officers' cap with khaki cover. The red staff brassard on his right sleeve shows 'L of C' lettering, denoting Lines of Communication. Brassards identified officers at the headquarters of a formation; red-blue for General Headquarters, red-black-red for Army, red-white-red for Corps, red for Division and blue for Brigade. Additional letters were worn to identify appointments. The photograph is dated March 1914.

Left: General Sir Edmund Ironside photographed whilst in Russia with the North Russian Relief Force. In October 1918, at the age of 38, Ironside was appointed Commander in Chief of the Archangel occupational force. He wears animal fur boots, leather jerkin with large toggles to aid fastening in cold weather and a seal-skin hat, proudly affixed with a general officers bullion badge.

Chaplain (4th Class) A.W. Boodle. In the British Army the chaplain was commonly called a "Padre". Ordained chaplains in the Army Chaplain's Department held relative ranks from captain to colonel. A captain was the equivalent of a Chaplain 4th Class.

Left: An Army Chaplain's Department Padre wearing standard officers SD with clerical 'dog' collar and ACD black Maltese cross insignia. Shoulder straps were edged in black to denote a chaplain to which rank insignia was worn. Chaplains of various denominations – e.g. Roman Catholic, Church of England, Presbyterian – played an important part not only in the spiritual but also in the material life of the troops.

Above: Lieutenant Godfrey-James, Young Men's Christian Association (YMCA) in a Burberrys 'Trench Coat'. The YMCA was founded in 1844, and during the 1914-1918 war setup a variety of huts, open free of charge to all regardless of religious belief. The photograph is dated January 1919.

Left: Reverend T/Chaplain to the Forces, T.B. Hardy VC, DSO, MC. Hardy was attached to the 8th Battalion, Lincolnshire Regiment, and died of wounds received in action. He won the Victoria Cross in April 1918 for attending to and rescuing wounded whilst under heavy fire. Army chaplains won a total of three VC's during the First World War.

Left: Lieutenant H. Hanley, YMCA wearing a standard field service officers KD jacket, Cairo 1917. By the end of the war the YMCA had opened up over 10,000 huts for servicemen, from luxurious clubs in the centre of Cairo to makeshift bars in France and Flanders offering cups of tea close to the front line.

Below left: An ASC officer with a French interpreter in Doullens, France, March 1916. Interpreters were attached to the British Army and were distinguishable by the Egyptian Sphinx interpreters' collar dogs.

Below: A Greek interpreter, attached to a London Regiment. Note the cap badge on the Wolseley Pattern helmet and the interpreter's red over white brassard. On the reverse of the postcard is written "Egypt, May 6th, 1917".

Opposite
An officer photographed in Arras with a French interpreter, who wears the Egyptian Sphinx interpreters' collar badge. The British officer wears a covered second issue steel helmet with a one-piece chinstrap and rimmed edge. He also wears a 'Trench Coat' and leather 'Stohwasser' leggings.

Chapter Three

Field Infantry Officers

A pre-war photograph of a South Staffordshire officer that clearly shows the closed stand and fall collar with bronzed 'collar dogs', and twisted drab cord shoulder straps. He is equipped with Sam Browne and Pattern 1892 Infantry Officer Sword.

Right: A pre-war photograph of an officer wearing an early cuff rank jacket with drab twisted cord shoulder straps, as introduced in 1904. In 1913 these were replaced with sewn down, plain cloth shoulder straps and an open stepped collar revealing the shirt and tie.

A York & Lancaster Regiment subaltern in 1914. He wears a Pattern 1913 cuff rank jacket with an open, step collar to reveal the shirt and tie. The trousers are made in a similar whipcord material to the jacket, and worn with field ankle boots. He is equipped with Sam Browne and Pattern 1892 Infantry Officer Sword.

An Honourable Artillery Company (HAC) officer, c.1914, wearing a shoulder rank jacket, similar to that worn by the guards and cavalry regiments. He is equipped in marching order double brace Sam Browne with a Royal Artillery Pattern Officer's Sword.

Battalion officers of the Hampshire Regiment photographed before leaving for France, 1914. The Sam Browne was originally designed to carry the officers' sword, pistol holster and ammunition pouch, but was soon used to carry a wide array of supplementary accoutrements that could be worn either on a belt loop e.g. binoculars and compass, or on short snap-hook straps e.g. haversack, map case and water bottle.

A group of officers from the Highland Light Infantry aboard a transport on their way to France. From the look of their uniforms and equipment the photograph probably dates from early 1915. Notice the officer who is still wearing the pre-war jacket with stand and fall collar and sewn down cloth shoulder straps.

A Gordon Highlander captain wearing the Scottish 'doublet' pattern of jacket with Gordon tartan trews. He wears 'Stohwasser' leather leggings that stayed popular throughout the war, even though puttees became the regulation wear.

Notts & Derby Regiment (Sherwood Foresters) officers in 1915. Some wear the Pattern 1914 Infantry Equipment with various officer accoutrements, including pistol holster, binocular, torch and map case.

Bombing officers from 15th (London Welsh) Royal Welsh Fusiliers in December 1915. They pose in shirt-sleeve order which shows details of the drab colored shirt with removable collar. Walking canes were a standard officer accessory of the time.

An officer from the 25th (Frontiersman) Royal Fusiliers in Pattern 1908 Infantry Equipment and Wolseley Pattern helmet with regimental badge. This unique Battalion was formed by the Legion of Frontiersman, a self-governing military organization that had been in existence since 1904.

Above: An atmospheric studio portrait of a 9th (Pioneers) Battalion, South Staffordshire Regiment officer. Note the ribbon of the Military Cross, the wound stripe and the crossed pick-axe and rifle pioneer collar badges. The battalion moved with the 23rd Division from France to Italy in November 1917.

Above right: A Notts & Derby Regiment (Sherwood Foresters) officer, believed to be Major B. W. Vann VC, MC & Bar. He is equipped with a set of Pattern 1908 equipment with pouches, a leather trench torch and pistol holster. Vann won his Victoria Cross on September 28th, 1918, but fell victim to an enemy sniper four days later.

Right: An officer wearing a 'LONDON WELSH' cloth patch on a 'wind-up' shoulder rank jacket. The London Welsh were largely recruited from Welsh men living in London, who made up the 15th Battalion, Royal Welsh Fusiliers. The photographed was taken in Poperinghe, and dated on the reverse March 14th, 1917.

Above left: Two officers from the 14th (Swansea) Battalion, Welsh Regiment in France. Note the man standing is wearing a blue cloth trench mortar trade badge on his upper arm. In December 1915 light trench mortar batteries, armed with Stokes, were under battalion level control, but moved under brigade command in March 1916.

Above: A captain and adjutant of the Worcestershire Regiment wearing an early pattern double-breasted greatcoat with turn-back cuffs. Ranking was worn on the shoulder straps rather than on the cuffs, with shoulder straps piped in arm-of-service colors, in this case it would be scarlet for the infantry. The photograph is marked "Xmas 1915".

Left: King's Own (Royal Lancaster Regiment) officers photographed in a studio at Poperinghe, otherwise known as 'Pop', near Ypres. On the back it says "Taken the day we last got out of the line" c.1917. The studio location is identified by the cloth backdrop depicting the ruined city of Ypres.

Above: Officers in different styled waterproof coats. These 'Trench Coats' or Macs were immensely popular with officers, famously the 'Burberrys' and the 'Mackintosh' designs.

Above right: Second-Lieutenant Arthur Spencer, York and Lancaster Regiment. He was killed at Ovillers on the Somme, July 1st, 1916. He is photographed wearing leather field service 'trench' boots and a private purchased Burberrys 'Trench Coat' with leather football buttons. He wears the winter service officer's trench cap with buckled neck flap.

Right: Trench coated officers photographed by a war-torn building. The officer in the middle is wearing the French 'Adrian' 1915 pattern helmet. Before the issue of the 'Brodie' steel helmet some British officers chose to wear the French pattern, one notable personality was Major, The Hon. Winston Churchill, who commanded the 6th Royal Scots Fusiliers in early 1916.

2nd Battalion, Welsh Regiment officers wearing a variety of 'Trench Coats' and a double-breasted wool coat with turned back cuffs. This semi-official short cut double-breasted coat had leather 'football' buttons, and was referred to as the 'British Warm'. Photographed in Rouen, May 1916.

An officer from the West Yorkshire Regiment in an officers style Gor'blimey winter service cap and 'British Warm' greatcoat.

Grenadier Guards officers in a trench, c.1915. Note the 'Orilux' trench torch holder on the officer's belt. Guards pattern jackets were shoulder rank, with their buttons arranged in a set order to distinguish the particular Guards Regiment.

An unusual, candle-lit photograph of South Staffordshire Regiment officers in a dugout. Note that two of the officers are wearing fleece coat liners that would button into a 'British Warm' or a 'Trench Coat' for extra warmth.

An officer in winter trench gear. On the reverse it says "On the Job! Everybody wears these boots in the trenches also either a fur-coat or a leather waistcoat". Goatskins, amongst other animal skins, were worn to help deal with the crippling cold of long winter days and nights.

Lieutenant Thomas Higginson, 3rd Battalion, Grenadier Guards, wearing the pattern of jacket unique to the Guards regiments. He also wears lace-up officers field service 'trench' boots, spurs and a small leather belt pouch that probably contains a jack-knife. Higginson was killed on September 15th, 1916. The photograph is dated February 6th, 1916.

Right: A lieutenant from the 1/6th (Morayshire) Battalion, Seaforth Highlanders, August 1915. The Balmoral bonnet had long tassels at the rear, also common to the Glengarry. On the latter issued Tam-o'-Shanter the tassels were permanently fastened at the back into a bow.

Below: 1/6th (Morayshire) Battalion, Seaforth Highlanders officers on the Somme, August 1915. The kilted officer wears a Scottish styled cuff rank 'doublet', Mackenzie tartan kilt and a drab colored bonnet. The other officer wears the earlier Pattern 1904 jacket, in doublet style, with twisted cord shoulder straps and closed stand and fall collar.

Below right: The Hunter brothers – Captain Hope Hunter, 2/14th (London Scottish) Battalion, London Regiment with his brother, a Sub-Lieutenant in the Royal Naval Division (RND). The photograph shows details of the Scottish and RND styles of officer jackets. On the back is written, "Death is swallowed up in Victory". Captain H. Hunter was killed on December 2nd, 1917.

With cane and pipe. Royal Scots officers relaxing out of the line, May 1917.

Above: Officers of 'A' Company, Drake Battalion 'HQ', RND. They are wearing the RND pattern jacket with rank on both shoulders and cuffs. The cuff rank, made of khaki or gold braid, is of the naval rank pattern. Note the naval caps with khaki covers. The rectangular blue battalion patch on the wooden sign denotes Drake Battalion.

Left: A captain in the Royal Marine Light Infantry (RMLI). The photograph is taken near Bully Grenay, Lens on August 25th, 1916. Officers of the RMLI, unlike their RND companions, wore the typical army cuff-rank jacket, as opposed to the naval RND pattern of jacket.

Opposite
Top left: Two officers from 19th (Glamorgan Pioneers) Battalion, Welsh Regiment, in France. Note the crossed pick-axe and rifle collar badges worn with their regimental collar dogs. The cloth sign bearing the Welsh dragon denotes the 38th (Welsh) Division. The photograph is dated January 11th, 1918.

Top right: Welsh officers from 115th Brigade, 38th (Welsh) Division. They are from 10th (1/Gwent) and 11th (2/Gwent) Battalion South Wales Borderers and the 16th (Cardiff City) Battalion, Welsh Regiment, taken in France on August 16th, 1916.

Bottom: Officers and sergeants of 'B' Company, 1/19th (St Pancras) Battalion, London Regiment. This photograph was taken at Les Brebis in January 1916, prior to the battalion taking over the Double Crassier sector at Loos. Captain Fox, the officer at the front, wears the short pattern rubber gum boots, as issued from trench stores.

A Royal Scots Fusilier officer holding his 'battle bowler', one of the nicknames for the British steel helmet. This is the Mark I pattern which began to appear during the latter half of 1916, distinguishable by the additional steel folded rim which made the edge less sharp. Other popular nicknames were 'trench hat', 'tin hat' and 'shrapnel helmet'.

A mud and chalk splattered officer in winter trench gear, posing with walking stick and pipe. This photograph was taken on the Somme during the winter fighting in late 1916.

Officers from the Oxfordshire and Buckinghamshire Light Infantry. Note the collar cords that were worn by this unit instead of metal collar badges.

A 12th (The Rangers) Battalion, London Regiment officer in Sam Browne order with binoculars, holster, ammunition pouch and 'PH' bag. Note the lace-up variety of trench boot with the buckled flaps. These were very popular with officers on active service.

Above: Second-Lieutenant Reginald Harry Talbot Croney, attached to 8th Battalion, North Staffordshire Regiment, who was killed on August 9th, 1918. This photograph was taken at Bully-Grenay near Lens in late 1916. Notice the helmet covers with painted North Staffordshire badges.

Top right: Northumberland Fusilier pioneer officers in Arras, c.1916. All wear steel helmets with bronzed regimental cap badges fixed to the cloth covers. The man in the middle is wearing a 'wind-up' jacket with shoulder rank whilst the others still wear the cuff rank. The major wears the ribbon of the Military Cross.

Right: An officer in Sam Browne 'marching order' that includes a revolver holster, haversack, water bottle, compass and map case. The box respirator satchel on his chest dates the photograph from autumn 1916.

Opposite
Top left: Two artillery officers. One wears the painted badge of the 58th (London) Division on his helmet, whilst the other has the cloth sign of the 47th (London) Division on his jacket. Note that both wear the mounted version of the box respirator satchel with modified shoulder strap.

Top right: A British officer from the 29th Division, note the red half-diamond divisional patch. He wears lace up style trench boots and has a sandbag covered helmet. Helmet covers were often privately purchased by the officers from outfitters like Hawkes & Co, or Woodrow of Piccadilly. The photograph is dated July 14th, 1917.

Bottom: Tyneside Scottish officers wearing a mixture of equipment, c.1917. In January 1915 an army order was published that stated that officers in the line were to be equipped with the same accoutrements as the rank and file. This aimed to make the officer less conspicuous in the field to the enemy marksmen.

Above: Scottish officers in France with their chaplain, Reverend David Scott. The lieutenant on the right with the Military Cross ribbon is wearing Pattern 1914 equipment with holster and ammunition pouch. The others wear a mix of webbing equipment with officer accoutrements.

Opposite
Top: A humorous photograph of officers from the 9th (Scottish) Division wearing each others headgear. By 1916 this division was made up from a mix of Scottish Highland and Lowland regiments as well as a South African Brigade.

Bottom: South Africans, Scots and Texans – a mix of officers, probably at training school in France 1918.

S. AFRICA
ROYAL SCOTS
TEXAS
ROYAL SCOTS
N.Z.

Chapter Four

Field Infantry

A 'Call to Arms'. Saying goodbye to his father. Note the muzzle cover on the 'long' Lee-Enfield rifle. It was standard practice for soldiers to take their rifle and pack with them on leave.

Above: A studio photograph taken in France of three soldiers wearing issue woolen cap comforters and cardigans. Carried in the large pack when not worn, many were sent to the troops as comfort fund gifts from loved ones and charities at home.

Left: For King and Country. Private T.A. Brown, MT-ASC leaving for the front December 12th, 1916. Note the box respirator and the details of the issued khaki mess-tin cover with loops to the front. Brown's name is stenciled on the kit bag, just visible in the foreground.

A draft from the 1/5th Battalion, Seaforth Highlanders before departing for France. Note the section marksman on the right who is armed with the accurate 303-inch Pattern 1914 'sniper' Rifle. The P14, or officially the No.3 Mk.I, was popular with marksman because of its accuracy. This Territorial unit wore the Sutherland tartan instead of the Seaforth Mackenzie tartan.

Above: Welsh Regiment other ranks in woolen cap comforters and light shaded cardigans. Note the aluminum identity disks being worn, as introduced in August 1906. Commonly called the 'dog-tag', the pattern was superseded in August 1914 with a red circular fibre disk, which in turn was replaced in August 1916 with a pair of dog tags, a green octagonal disk and a red circular disk.

Below: Soldiers in shirt-sleeve working order, showing details of the grey-back flannel shirt, braces and stable-belts. Note the single fibre identity disk being worn by one man, and the aluminum disk by another. This *Carte Postale* was sent June 21st, 1915.

"Halt, Who goes there?" A Territorial Royal Welsh Fusilier with a 'long' Lee-Enfield rifle and the first issue Pattern 1908 haversack that was similar in style to the Pattern 1903 canvas haversack. This pattern was superseded in 1909 with the Pattern 1908 webbing version.

Private Dick Wallis, 'B' Company, 1st Battalion, Bedfordshire Regiment in 'Full Service Marching Order'. Wallis was killed on the Somme on September 5th, 1916. Note the wristwatch, sometimes called a wristlet, which became popular wear during the Great War.

A lance-corporal from 2nd Battalion, Argyll and Sutherland Highlanders, dated August 30th, 1916. He wears a khaki apron to protect and subdue his kilt, a Balmoral bonnet and 'PH' gas hood bag. Notice the No.1 Mark 1 breech cover on his SMLE, which was introduced in June 1915.

Lance-Corporal Scantlebury, 28th (Artist Rifles) Battalion, London Regiment in marching order. He wears Pattern 1914 Infantry Equipment, map and binocular case. Note the cloth *Fleur-de-Lys* scout proficiency badge, sewn above the lance-corporal chevrons.

Private Frank Shepherd, Royal Fusiliers in Pattern 1914 Infantry Equipment with a 'Gor'blimey' winter service dress cap. Note the unusual shaped water bottle. These were manufactured by the Canadian Aluminum Goods Company in 1914/1915 to help with the general equipment shortages in Britain during the early part of the war.

An East Yorks corporal with his kit layout c.1916. From top to bottom: Pattern 1914 equipment, SD cap, cardigan, SD jacket and trousers, greatcoat, blanket, holdall, socks, shirts, mess-tin with cover, scarf, gloves, housewife, boots, brushes and bayonet.

Men of the King's (Liverpool Regiment) in camp. They show the Pattern 1914 Infantry Equipment in 'Full Service Marching Order' with the Small Box Respirator (SBR) carried on the chest, c.1917.

Men of the 1/2nd Battalion, Monmouthshire Regiment in camp. They wear Pattern 1914 equipment with modified double strap pouches, as introduced in 1917. The double strap variety was designed to help add extra security to the pouch fastening to prevent loss of ammunition; however by this stage of the war, webbing was in adequate supply to replace what leather equipment still remained in the field.

A Northumberland Fusilier sergeant in Pattern 1914 'marching order'. The puggaree with the red cloth band denotes this particular unit. The water bottle is the pattern made by the Canadian Aluminum Goods Company Ltd. and sold to Britain during the early years of the war.

The 1/1st Lanarkshire Yeomanry, part of the Lowland Mounted Brigade, departing for Gallipoli, July 1915. All are wearing drab serge service dress with newly issued Wolseley Pattern helmets. Note the mixture of accoutrements including wire cutters and binoculars.

A draft from the 9th Battalion, Royal Scots, photographed at Selkirk on April 20th, 1916. They are wearing a mixture of headdress including the smaller Balmoral bonnet, with and without drab cover, as issued in the spring of 1915. Some are also wearing the larger and floppier styled Tam-o'-Shanter which began to be issued in 1916. Wearing the 'Hunting Stuart' tartan beneath their kilt covers, the "Dandy Ninth" was the only Royal Scots battalion to wear the kilt.

Top left: A sergeant from a rifle regiment at Ras El Ain, Palestine, May 1st, 1918. The pattern of Khaki Drill (KD) jacket (frock) is of a simplified pattern with basic stand collar, pointed pocket flaps and plain cuffs. Note the black buttons that denote a rifle regiment.

Above: A stretcher-bearer from the 10th Battalion, Devonshire Regiment, 26th Division. This photograph was taken on active service in Salonika, 1917. The slouch hat, often associated with the Australians, was also issued in large numbers to the British for wear in tropical climates.

Left: Sergeant-Major E.R. Hart, 1/1st Scottish Horse. The Scottish Horse fought with distinction at Gallipoli, Egypt, Macedonia and in France and Flanders. Note the pattern of service dress jacket that was unique to this unit.

Opposite
Top: Royal Naval Division (RND) ratings at Crystal Palace in early 1915. They wear the standard issue blue naval uniform with high canvas gaiters and naval leather equipment. The RND began to be issued their army uniform in early 1915.

Bottom: Royal Naval Division wearing the drab serge naval caps with RND tallies. The black cap tally bared the legend 'ROYAL NAVAL DIVISION' in gold lettering. All are wearing puttees, instead of the naval gaiters. Note the red on khaki fouled anchor cloth badge that denotes the naval rank of leading seaman.

ROYAL NAVAL DIVISION
83.

An RND man wearing the army drab serge simplified jacket and trousers together with the short-lived drab serge peak-less naval cap. Photographed in 1915 at Blandford Camp, England before their departure to Gallipoli.

Petty Officer William Johnston served with Drake and Anson Battalions, and died as a sub-lieutenant in a POW camp in November 1918. Note the bomber's badge on his lower right arm, Petty Officer red on khaki crossed fouled anchors and the RND shoulder title being worn as a cap badge. c. 1915.

From sailor to soldier. A RND group wearing both naval and army SD caps. When the RND became part of the Army's 63rd (Royal Naval) Division the Pattern 1905 SD cap became common wear, but it was not until 1916 that the RND were issued individual battalion cap badges.

"Bob in the middle" Old Contemptibles in the trenches, late 1914. Note the trench periscope and spare small-arms ammunition (SAA) bandoliers at the ready. The phrase 'old contemptible' was taken from the Kaiser's early war comments on Britain's "contemptible little army".

"One of my Sergeants" A sergeant from the Essex Regiment, spring 1915. He wears a woolen cap comforter, commonly gifts from loved ones or fund raisers at home, who knitted and sent items including socks, scarves, body belts and waistcoats to the men in the trenches.

Top left: "On the lookout in the firing line" Men from the Essex Regiment in the trenches, early 1915. Note the trench periscope attached to the front of the trench, called the parapet. The reverse of the trench was called the parados.

Above: "Two of my NCO's in the firing line" Men from the Essex Regiment in the trenches, early 1915. Note the woolen cap comforters and the hook quillon Pattern 1907 bayonet. The hook quillon on the cross-guard was dispensed with from 1913.

Left: Lieutenant E.J.M. Robertson, 70th Battery RFA in a trench manned by the Kings Royal Rifle Corps. Robertson was killed at Festubert on May 22nd, 1915. He is wearing a 'British Warm' whilst the sentry is dressed in an early issue great-coat and wears a Balaclava helmet with his cap to help protect against the cold.

Opposite
Top: "In trenches at Festubert, March 21st, 1915".

Bottom: Tommy's in a winter dugout, equipment and rifles at the ready.

Left: A marksman poses with rifle at the ready. This is almost certainly a staged photograph, that also shows an officer standing below with a .455-inch Webley Mark IV service revolver. Notice both men have removed their puttees.

Above: A soldier wrapped up warmly in an animal fur coat and Gor'blimey with foul weather cover. 'Wooly Bears', also nicknamed 'Teddy-bears' and 'Stinkers' became popular during the first winters of the war until adequate supplies of leather jerkins became available.

Left: Men from 1/6th Battalion, Seaforth Highlanders in a Somme trench, August 1915. All wear the simplified jacket without the highland cut away front. An Army Order in 1915 ordered this alteration to be stopped as it was felt that rounding the skirts was unnecessary in wartime, as sporrans were no longer worn in the field. Note the observer with binoculars has the summer issue neck curtain attached to his bonnet.

1/6th Seaforths in a trench, August 1915. Note the observer looking through the trench periscope has a 'PH' gas hood bag. They are armed with the 'long' Lee-Enfield with the Pattern 1888 short bayonet, as used in the Boer War. By the closing months of 1915 sufficient stocks of SMLE's with Pattern 1907 bayonets were available for their replacement.

Marked on the back "Taken Boxing Day – Somewhere in France – 'B' Coy. Officers Mess Servants, 1/1st Cambridgeshire Regt., BEF, France (Flixecourt, Somme)". The 1/1st Battalion acted as a Training Battalion during this period for the Third Army School at Flixecourt until February 1916 when it became part of 118th Brigade, 39th Division. All wear the Gor'blimey except one who wears a forage cap.

A kilted soldier from the Liverpool Scottish in fur coat, Glengarry, apron kilt cover and Pattern 1908 webbing. Note the early issue No.1 Mark III SMLE with magazine cut-off and long range volley sight graduated for 1,600 to 2,800 yards. The No.1 Mark III* SMLE, as approved in January 1916, dispensed with both the cut-off and the volley sight.

Going into the line – a York and Lancaster Regiment private looking warmly wrapped up in his long-sleeved wooly bear 'stinker'. Armed with an SMLE, his Pattern 1914 equipment is just visible.

Left: A North Staffordshire Other Rank in winter issued 'wooly bear', Gor'blimey and thigh-length rubber waders. 'Gum' boots were manufactured by various rubber companies in Britain, and kept in 'Trench Stores' for frontline issue.

Gordon Highlanders photographed against a popular backdrop in Arras, 1917. Both are wearing Tam-o'-Shanters and are protected from the cold by sleeveless 'wooly bears'. The man on the right has one wound stripe and a colored band on his lower left-hand sleeve. A red band denoted a runner, green a scout, yellow a carrying party and blue a signaler.

An Argyll and Sutherland Highlander in a wooly bear 'stinker'. The sheep or goatskin coats were great on a cold and frosty morning, however when it rained, they became a smelly and sodden burden.

SB
SB

1916 "10th" GLoster"
Stretcher Bearers

Right: Signalers from 11th (Lonsdale) Battalion, Border Regiment on the Somme, 1916. They were formed in Penrith on September 17th, 1914 by the Earl of Lonsdale and an Executive Committee. The Battalion lost heavily on July 1st, 1916 and by May 1918 it was reduced to cadre strength.

Below: 1/23rd (County of London) Battalion, London Regiment at Verquin, a popular billet, June 1915. Note the neck sun curtains. These were authorized issued in June 1915 and used to help protect the neck from the sun. They were worn from the Middle-East to the Western Front.

Opposite
Top: A Northumberland Fusilier stretcher-bearer section. Nearly all wear pre-war manufactured Pattern 1908 webbing. The man, front right, is wearing unmodified ammunition pouches and also the first issue shoulder braces. These are distinguishable by the straight tab ends and flared shoulders.

Bottom: "10th Gloster Stretcher-Bearers, France 1916". Five of the men at the front are wearing field modified Gor'blimey caps with the neck flaps removed. This appears to be a fairly common practice during this mid-war period.

Men from 'D' Company, 8th Battalion, Royal Sussex Regiment in 1916. This battalion served as Pioneers for the 18th Division. Most are wearing the summer issue neck curtains on their SD caps, as officially authorized in June 1915.

Royal Sussex Regiment in France, early 1916. Note the gunners in the front wearing pistol kit, whilst the others wear a mix of Pattern 1908 and 1914 equipment. Lewis guns were supplied to the army from July 1915; originally four guns per battalion, but by July 1918, each battalion had thirty-six guns.

A Northumberland Fusiliers (Pioneer) Battalion, Machine Gun Section in France. Note the 'MG' skill-at-arms badge and pioneer cross pick-axe and rifle collar dogs on the jackets. Pioneer machine-gun sections spent a great deal of their time on detachment, also forming Anti-Aircraft defense for Divisional HQ. The photograph is dated April 16th, 1916.

The Machine Gun Section of 1/6th Battalion, Black Watch "Somewhere in France 1915". By February 1915 each battalion had four Vickers guns allocated per battalion, until they were withdrawn and replaced by Lewis guns when the MGC was created in October 1915. Notice that very few have the front skirts of their jackets tailored back, as stopped by an Army Order in 1915. Many are also wearing the short lived drab Balmoral bonnet.

A group of men from the Gloucestershire Regiment in France, c.1915. All wear the winter service Gor'blimey caps, as issued during the first winter of the war, and equipped with Pattern 1914 Infantry Equipment.

A Gloucestershire Regiment Headquarters Section, c.1916. Note the Model 'D', Mark III Field Telephones, cable and sighting telescopes in the foreground. The D III became an essential piece of communications equipment for all arms in forward areas.

DCLI sergeants "Somewhere in France". The sergeant sitting on the right is wearing a cloth 'Cornwall' regimental patch and also a bomber's badge. Note the Gor'blimey's and Pattern 1905 caps, with and without foul weather covers.

East Kent Regiment (Buffs) stretcher-bearers in France, late 1916. Note the 'SB' cut down and sewn onto the jacket arms, instead of the standard armband that stretcher-bearers normally wore. 'SB' brassards were worn by individuals in infantry regiments, mostly bandsmen, who acted as stretcher-bearers to help the RAMC bring casualties in from the front.

A Rifle Brigade group in 'Full Service Marching Order', c.1918. They have box respirators worn on top of the large pack with the strap secured to the front of the waist belt. This was a popular way to carry the gas mask satchel when on the march.

Grenadier Guards in camp near Ypres. Most have red cloth shoulder titles with 'GRENADIER GUARDS' titled in white. A few are wearing Gor'blimey's whilst the others are wearing SD caps, with and without the neck curtain. The photograph is dated May 28th, 1916.

Sergeant J. Bernard MM, 11th Battalion, Royal Scots, 9th (Scottish) Division. He is wearing Pattern 1908 Infantry Equipment in 'battle order' without the large pack. Note the divisional sign of a small Scottish silver thistle, placed on a blue circle, as introduced in 1918 for wear on the uniform.

A North Staffordshire Regiment warrant officer (WO) wearing a Pattern 1908 belt with cut-down pouches for his revolver ammunition, attached unorthodoxly to the shoulder braces. The rank crown on the left sleeve denotes a WOII Class or CSM (Company Sergeant Major). Note the issue pattern of uniform cut into the officer style.

Right: A soldier from the Army Cyclist Corps poses with a rabbit. He wears specialist cyclists' knickerbockers, or shorts that were first issued in July 1915. These were made out of drab serge and manufactured with a reinforced padded seat for comfort.

A Royal Fusilier in 1915 'battle order' sometimes referred to as 'fighting kit'. Notice the sandbags tied to the shoulder braces and an emergency ration bag fastened to his belt. This is the equipment he would have worn for going 'over the top'. Note also the neck curtain and early production left-hand pouch without the strap modification.

Two soldiers from the 1/1st Buckinghamshire Battalion in marching order. One wears a fur coat under the SD jacket, whilst the other soldier wears a leather jerkin, also beneath his service dress. The photograph dates from winter 1916.

Above: A raggedy group of men from the Duke of Wellington Regiment after coming out of the trenches. Note the corporal with the trench whistle and binoculars, and also the leather jerkins, worn over and under the jackets. The photograph is dated March 9th, 1917.

Opposite
Top: HQ Company, 8th Battalion, Somerset Light Infantry, 37th Division in France 1916. A Headquarters Company encompassed the battalions transport and administrative elements, as well as signalers, scouts, runners and other specialists.

Bottom: "5th Platoon, 'B' Company, 1/1st Buckinghamshire Battalion – The Fighting Fifth". Photographed in a French farm courtyard, they are equipped in a mix of Pattern 1908 and 1914 equipment, typical of the mid-war period when supplies of either patterns were in short supply.

H.Q. Coy
6th Som.L.I.

5 PLATOON
B Coy
1/1 BUCKS
The Fighting Fifth

A studio portrait of a Northamptonshire soldier which shows close up detail of the Pattern 1905 SD cap with its thin brown leather chinstrap. He also wears a dismounted pattern drab serge greatcoat with its single brass collar hook.

A South Staffordshire Other Rank wearing a late pattern greatcoat without turned back cuffs, as introduced in 1917. His set of Pattern 1908 just fits over the greatcoat, with the belt adjusted to its maximum limit. The belts were issued in three sizes: small, medium and large.

A soldier and sapper in mounted pattern greatcoats with drab serge soft caps, photographed in Poperinghe 1917. 'Pop', an ancient Belgian town situated south of the province of West Flanders, was the primary military centre for the British Army located in Flanders, just under 10km west of Ypres.

Above: A soldier of the Rifle Brigade wearing a rubberized coat, whilst his Lincoln's colleague is wearing an earlier variation of the dismounted pattern greatcoat with rifle patches and diagonal buttoned chest pockets.

Above right: A Scots Guards warrant officer, photographed in a studio at 120 Princes Street in Edinburgh. Note the khaki covered blue bonnet with an officer's quality cap badge.

Right: A sergeant from the 1/25th (Cyclist) Battalion, London Regiment wearing standard service dress with Sam Browne belt and a 'Mackintosh Cape'. The cape was introduced in late 1914 and universally issued to troops, albeit in limited numbers, until superseded by the groundsheet cape in 1917.

Left: The Mackintosh cape being worn by a trooper from the 13th Hussars. The cape was made of a waterproofed Mackintosh material with collar, button front and slots on either side for the arms. The cape could be fastened by buttons at the front, or simply worn off the shoulders by the provision of two interior straps.

Two dispatch riders on active service. One is wearing the mounted pattern greatcoat whilst the other is wearing a rubberized waterproofed Sou'wester style coat. Both are also wearing the short pattern rubber gum boots. The steel helmets and gas mask satchels dates the photo around 1917.

Opposite
A corporal in greatcoat marching order. He wears a full set of Pattern 1914 Infantry Equipment and a helmet with a pull-string cover. The small box respirator is worn on the chest in the alert position.

A South Staffordshire Regiment Other Rank in marching order. He wears a two-piece sacking cover on his helmet with a painted regimental sign. Note also the peg variety of ammunition pouch, which uses brass posts instead of poppers for closing the flaps. These were supplied in small numbers from 1915 onwards.

A mud-splattered Tommy in 'battle order'. Battle order in July 1916 consisted of two gas hoods, commonly a 'Hypo' helmet and a 'PH' helmet, a mess-tin, haver-sack with iron rations, steel helmet, filled water bottle, two SAA bandoliers of 100 rounds, a waterproof sheet, two sandbags and two Mills bombs. The reverse of the card is written "Taken in France, 1916".

A soldier from the 17th (3rd Glasgow Pals) Battalion, Highland Light Infantry on the Somme, July 1916. They formed part of the 32nd Division, which was known to the Germans as the 'Red Division' because of the scheme of battle patches that were cut out of red cloth. On his arm you can see a cloth circle with four bars that denotes this battalion.

Corporal J.G. Oliver in France, 1916. He is equipped with Pattern 1914 'pistol kit', common to machine-gunners, that comprises of pistol holster and ammunition pouch instead of the standard pair of pouches. He also wears shorts, as cut down from service dress trousers, which during the summer months on the Western Front became hugely popular until discouraged and finally prohibited by a General Routine Order in October 1916.

Left: Two men from the 9th Battalion, East Surrey Regiment, 24th Division, after coming out of the line. Both wear Pattern 1908 equipment and have their helmets covered in sacking material. Covers were worn to eliminate reflection and help camouflage the wearer. Covering the helmet in mud was also a common solution until finishes were produced in a non-reflective paint.

A Tommy wearing a set of Pattern 1908 that includes the first issue left-hand pouch with straight tab ends and unmodified pockets. This pattern was modified in October 1914 to include a more secure opening system as a result of concerns about the loss of ammunition by troops at the front. This loss was caused inadvertently when troops leant on the trench walls to fire, catching and opening the lower three pockets.

Left: With pipe and rifle. Two men from the 6th Battalion, Royal Irish Regiment, 16th (Irish) Division, photographed near the frontline. They both have covers on their rifles to protect against the mud. Many covers were improvised from old socks and sacking, and it was not until mid-1915 that the 'Cover, breech, Mark I' was officially issued.

A soldier in Pattern 1914 Infantry Equipment in 'battle order' with the haversack fastened to the back in lieu of the large pack. He also wears a leather jerkin and carries a box respirator, c.1918. Notice the wound stripe, overseas stripes and unit 'battle patch' insignia.

A humorous, almost stage like, photograph of a soldier in marching order, with a waterproof groundsheet just visible under the flap of the large pack. Note the rifle breech cover used to keep out the dirt.

Work horses of the BEF. Pioneer battalions were created in 1914 as a new concept in the British Army, intended to provide the Royal Engineers with skilled labor and to relieve the infantry from some of its non-combatant duties. About fifty percent of pioneers worked with GS pick and shovel whilst the others had a recognized trade with skills ranging from joiners and masons, to bricklayers and blacksmiths.

Men, from possibly the 24th Division (note the insignia) pose for the photograph taken at Bully-Grenay in 1917. Two are wearing the winter issue leather jerkins, common issue from 1916 onwards, and rough field-made sandbag helmet covers.

An atmospheric studio portrait of a battle-hardened soldier just out of the line. He is armed with a SMLE with fixed Pattern 1907 bayonet. Protected from the cold by an issue leather jerkin with blanket lining, he also wears a greatcoat, home knitted woolen scarf and a mud-splattered steel helmet.

Chapter Five

Dominion Troops

Private R.G. Shearer, 4th Battalion, Australian Imperial Force (AIF), who was killed at Lone Pine, Gallipoli on August 7th, 1915. He wears the Australian Service Dress Jacket, fur-felt slouch hat and early unmodified Pattern 1908 pouches. He is armed with a No.1 Mk.III SMLE rifle and early Pattern 1907 hooked quillon bayonet.

An Australian wearing the Pattern 1908/15 Infantry Equipment, photographed in Australia. Some of this equipment did find its way to the battlefields, where it was worn in action on the Somme in 1916.

Australians at Camp 25, Larkhill on Salisbury Plain, England. This photograph clearly shows the webbing Pattern 1908 Infantry Equipment in marching order, with details of the haversack and the water bottle carrier.

A Fourth Division Australian wearing a British Pattern 1902 SD jacket with Pattern 1908 equipment, a sacking covered helmet, and armed with a SMLE and Pattern 1907 bayonet. The postcard is dated July 1918. British pattern jackets were worn when there were supply shortages of the Australian service dress.

Left: Private Arthur Norman, 39th Battalion, AIF, with the greatcoat carried rolled in bandolier style c.1916. He wears the Australian version of the British SD cap which had a distinctive leather trimmed peak. He is also issued with the slouch hat, as adopted by Australia in the 1890s.

Above: An early 1915 photograph of a soldier in Brisbane, wearing the Australian SD cap with leather trimmed peak. The standard rising sun badge is worn. The cap was soon popularly superseded by the fur-felt slouch hat.

Above right: A beautifully lit studio portrait of an AIF soldier in the early leather peaked SD cap, as introduced pre-war, and a greatcoat bearing a First Division cloth patch.

Right: A CSM photographed in France, November 1916 wearing the Australian pattern greatcoat with rank insignia on the arm. The Australian greatcoat was similar to the British pattern, but commonly worn with horn buttons.

Left: A fine portrait photograph of a Gallipoli veteran wearing the DCM. Gallipoli veterans wore an 'A' for ANZAC on their cloth unit patches as an honor for service during the campaign.

A signaler in France, c.1917/18 wearing a British made jacket and hat. Note that the hat has a folded puggaree as opposed to the plain woolen band, more often than not a sign of British manufacture. The slouch hat was officially called 'Hat, khaki, Fur Felt', and commonly made of either rabbits fur or wool felt.

Left: 'Diggers' wearing the slouch hat and the Pattern 1905 SD cap. Notice the cloth unit patch behind the cap badge. The term 'digger' became common usage by the end of 1917, originating from the New Zealanders who took it from their country's gum-diggers. The Australians soon adopted the term, so then both Australian and New Zealander called each other digger.

Right: Third Australian Division diggers in their baggy styled woolen drab jackets. Men from this division are distinguishable by the left side of the hat being turned down along with the badge at the front, done to help establish an *esprit de corps*.

An Australian artilleryman photographed at Vignacourt in France. The standard Pattern 1903 bandolier is worn along with a pair of other ranks mounted pattern 'trench' boots. Interestingly he is wearing a Pattern 1908 shoulder brace as a walking-out belt.

Right: An officer from the 2nd Battalion, AIF in 1917. He appears to be wearing the medal ribbon for the 1911 Coronation. He wears the standard officer jacket with bronzed collar dogs, rank pips and 'AUSTRALIA' titles on the shoulders. Battalion patch insignia is just visible on the arms.

Above: Australians from the Third Division at rest near Ypres, 1917. All are wearing the Australian SD Jacket, with and without belt with standard cord breeches. The two sitting wear the signalers crossed flags proficiency badge on their left sleeve, over a blue signalers cuff band.

Below: An early photograph taken in 1915 of an Australian machine-gunner, armed with the Pattern 1901 303-inch Maxim machine-gun and standard wartime Mk.IV tripod mount.

'A' Section, 13th Machine Gun Company, AIF taken somewhere in France, December 6th, 1917. This section is armed with the Vickers machine-gun, which started replacing the heaver brass-jacketed Maxim at the beginning of the war.

Trooper Eric Billingshurst, 3rd Australian Light Horse Regiment, May 1915. The ALH left their horses in Egypt before proceeding to Gallipoli, in May 1915, where they fought as infantry.

Australian Light Horse (ALH) trooper, wearing a slouch hat with the distinctive ALH Emu feather. He also wears the Pattern 1903 bandolier, mounted pattern cord breeches with 'Stohwasser' leggings. Note the wristwatch. The Light Horse Brigade distinguished itself in the famous charge at Beersheba in 1917.

Australian Light Horse trooper in slouch hat with a set of Pattern 1903 Bandolier equipment. Note the early hook quillon Pattern 1907 bayonet and leather covered wristwatch. The photograph is dated October 31, 1915.

Imperial Camel Corps (ICC) trooper in shirt-sleeve order, lightly equipped with a Pattern 1903 bandolier, SMLE and Wolseley helmet. The ICC was formed as mounted infantry in Egypt in January 1916. Four battalions were eventually raised; 1st and 3rd were entirely Australian, 2nd was British, and the 4th was a mix of Australians and New Zealanders. The ICC also had its own machine-gun unit, and a battery of light artillery.

Trooper John Connew, 18th Company, 1st Battalion, ICC. Operations in the Western Desert in 1916 were characterized by long patrols and brief skirmishes with the Senussi tribesmen and eventually with the Turkish army. The battalions fought alongside ALH units at Romani, Magdhaba and Rafa. The ICC remained an integral part of the British and Dominion force that advanced through Palestine in 1917 and 1918, suffering particularly heavy casualties during the Second Battle of Gaza.

Diggers from the Fifth Australian Division with their Lewis Gunners and French Interpreter in France, 1918.

Private J. Rowley, 6th Wellington Mounted Rifles, NZEF is photographed in a 'hall of mirrors' which shows detailed views of the Australian type slouch hat. The distinctive 'lemon-squeezer' hat, instituted by Lt.Col. William Malone, became the national symbol of the New Zealand soldier. Later on in 1916 Major General Godley sent a directive that all NZ units to wear this hat in an effort to standardize headdress. This photograph is dated February 2nd, 1916.

Above: New Zealand Rifle Brigade 'kiwi' wearing the Pattern 1905 SD cap with a unit patch behind. He wears a NZ manufactured Pattern 1902 SD jacket that differs slightly in the way the rifle patches were finished closer to the patch pockets. The jacket has plain bone buttons.

Above right: A trooper from the Otago Mounted Rifles, NZEF wearing the distinctive Mounted Rifles Bandolier Equipment. It was a harness type, locally manufactured and unique to New Zealand, designed to restrict excessive movement and to prevent possible loss of ammunition when riding or in action. By 1918 this equipment was discarded in favor of the Pattern 1903 Bandolier Equipment.

Right: A New Zealand lance-corporal, probably of Maori origin, poses for a studio portrait. He is wearing a British simplified jacket with fern-leaf NZ badges. The fern-leaf badge led the New Zealanders to be nicknamed the 'fernleafs'. They were also called 'Anzacs', 'Diggers' and 'En-Zedders'.

Left: A New Zealand Medical Corps soldier with colored edge shoulder strap. The system of colored straps in the NZ forces was obsolete by 1916.

New Zealand Engineer 'Tunneller'. He wears a 'NZE' badged fur-felt 'kiwi' hat with colored puggaree. The band for the NZ Engineers was khaki, dark blue, khaki.

Left: A New Zealand Field Artillery bombardier with 'NZFA' metal titles over cloth shoulder strips, which probably denotes the battery. The photograph is dated October 23rd, 1918.

Left: New Zealand Field Artillery officers in France. All are wearing the standard cuff-rank jacket with their distinctive 'kiwi' hats with colored puggaree (dark blue, scarlet, dark blue). Note the old lady laughing from the background window.

Private Victor Webb, 28th (Saskatchewan) Battalion, Canadian Expeditionary Force (CEF), wearing Pattern 1899 'Oliver' Valise Equipment and carries a Canadian Ross Rifle. Webb was killed on April 6th, 1916 at St Eloi, near Ypres. This pattern of equipment was worn by the First Canadian Contingent during 1914 and 1915 before being replaced with Pattern 1908.

Left: New Zealand Headquarters personnel pose with a souvenir Baden Regimental Pickelhaube, photographed in Arras, September 13th, 1916. Note the peg variation of the Pattern 1908 pouch, whilst the SMLE in the foreground is protected by a No.1 Mk.I breech cover and a metal foresight protector.

The same corporal is now photographed in battle order, "Somewhere in France". He now wears a steel shrapnel helmet and the box respirator in the alert position. Note the early Pattern 1907 'sword' bayonet with hook quillon fixed on the SMLE.

Right: A corporal from the 27th Battalion, CEF in marching order. This battalion was part of the Second Canadian Division, and wore the battle patch of a blue circle above a blue square. He wears a soft cap and carries a steel helmet and small box respirator on his back.

Above: A Canadian from the 79th Battalion, CEF wearing the Pattern 1916 'Dismounted' Equipment. This modified version of the Oliver equipment was introduced into service in 1916 but did not last long when it was replaced by Pattern 1908.

Above right: A studio portrait of Private W.A. Terry, CEF wearing a stiffened Gor'blimey cap and a Canadian seven-button SD Jacket. Soft caps were sometimes smartened up by using wire stiffeners for studio portraits and parades, a practice lost when in the line.

Right: A Canadian 'old sweat', looking like Bruce Bairnsfather's famous 'Old Bill' character. He is wearing the British Pattern 1902 jacket and Gor'blimey cap. He wears three overseas stripes, a long service good conduct chevron and a wound stripe, c.1918.

Above: A soldier from the 1st Canadian Overseas Railway Construction Battalion, dated February 5th, 1917. He is wearing the Canadian Pattern 1903 SD jacket with the Canadian version of the Gor'blimey winter service cap. This hat is distinguishable by the way the fold-down flaps button together at the front.

Above right: With helmet and pipe. The practice of drilling holes in the helmet for attaching badges was banned in a wartime routine order as it weakened the structural integrity of the helmet. The practice seemed to have continued though, as this 1918 dated photograph shows.

Right: An NCO wearing the Canadian Pattern 1903 SD jacket and what appears to be a cut down Gor'blimey. He wears mounted pattern 'pantaloon' breeches and puttees worn in the mounted style with the tapes tied at the ankle. He holds a fired 18-pounder shrapnel shell.

Left: Three Canadian signalers, France 1917. They wear the Pattern 1902 SD and carry 'PH' gas hood bags. Note the Pattern 1908 brace straps being used as walking-out belts. All three are wearing crossed flag proficiency badges that denote qualified signalers.

A Canadian Scottish (Gordon Highlanders) sergeant in France. Note the traditional Scottish pattern of Glengarry and badge, the Pattern 1902 SD jacket with brass General Service 'CANADA' maple-leaf collar badges and colored shoulder straps. He also wears the ribbon for the Indian General Service Medal (1895-1902).

Left: 42nd (Royal Highlanders of Montreal) Battalion, CEF. The Canadians, as did the South African's, had their own kilted regiments, largely recruited from Scottish immigrants living in the country.

Right: Canadians in the mounted pattern and Canadian version of the dismounted pattern greatcoat. As with the Canadian SD jackets, both the mounted and dismounted patterns of greatcoat had extra buttons, a distinguishing feature when compared to the British pattern.

A Canadian wearing the Canadian mounted pattern greatcoat, unique to the CEF. The Pattern 1905 SD cap, protected by an oilskin cover, is worn the Canadian General Service maple-leaf badge.

Right: Two men from the Newfoundland Regiment. The man on the left is wearing a private purchase jacket, almost of officer quality material with tailored pocket flaps. Newfoundland was an independent British colony until 1949 when it became a province of Canada. The Newfoundland Contingent reached Britain in October 1914, and as part of the British 29th Division fought at Gallipoli and the Somme. The regiment was granted the title of 'Royal' in 1917 for recognition of its conduct in the defense of Masnieres.

4th (Scottish) Battalion, South African Infantry, joined the 9th (Scottish) Division in May 1916. The first major action of the South African's was at Delville Wood on the Somme when, on July 15th 1916, they captured a substantial part of the wood and put up an epic stand again fierce enemy counter-attacks. The South African Scottish wore the tartan of the Atholl Murrays.

A South African Heavy Artillery gunner in a South African pattern of jacket. Just over 136,000, twenty percent of the countries white male population saw active service in the British cause. The South African Brigade formed part of the 9th (Scottish) Division.

Left: A South African sergeant with three native laborers. The South African Native Labour Corps came to France in early 1917, and established its base at Arques-la-Bataille. Due to the shortage of manpower, the demand was filled by importing men from China, India, South Africa, Egypt and other places within the British Empire. By the wars end some 300,000 total laborers had been employed, of whom nearly 200,000 were on the Western Front. There were over 90,000 non-white South African's serving in various theatres of war.

Wounded Indians convalescing. All wear the turban or 'Pagri' headdress tied in the manner of each mans race. Two of the greatcoats are the early pattern with shoulder rifle patches and small 'ticket' pockets. The man on the right is wearing a 'hospital' coat.

A 'bomber' from the British West Indies Regiment (BWIR), photographed in Egypt, February 1st, 1918. In 1915 the BWIR was formed from local volunteers to fight overseas. There was widespread enthusiasm on the islands to help the war effort, and the cost of sending the regiment to France was raised from public subscription. Two thirds of the total recruitment of 15,200 was Jamaican, though each of the colonies sent volunteers.

Above: A group photograph of BWIR men with Royal Engineers. The regiment saw service in East Africa, Egypt, Palestine, Jordan, France and Italy. Two battalions were involved in fighting against the Turks in Palestine and Jordan in 1918, however the War Office considered later that colonial troops should not be fighting against Europeans. Consequently the remaining battalions were employed as native labor battalions – carrying ammunition, digging trenches and gun emplacements, often under heavy enemy bombardments.

Below: Indian Mobile Veterinary Section, Army Veterinary Corps, dated February 6th, 1915. Wounded or sick animals were initially treated by the mobile section at divisional level, and evacuated back, if necessary, to specialist veterinary hospitals at the rear. The AVC was granted the title of 'Royal', *vide* Army Order 362 of 1918 for services during the war.

Above: Indian POW's in German captivity. India sent 140,000 men to the Western Front, 90,000 in the Indian Army and the Indian Cavalry Corps, and 50,000 in labor companies. The photo shows a Havildar (Sergeant), a Lance Naik (Lance Corporal) and a Sepoy (Private).

Below: Sowars (troopers) of the 34th Prince Albert Victor's Own Poona Horse resting on the Somme, August 1915. This unit served in France from October 1914 until February 1918 when they were dispatched to join General Allenby's forces in Palestine. Amongst their battle honors are: 'LA BASSEE 1914', 'ARMENTIERES 1914', 'SOMME 1916' 'FLERS-COURCELETTE 1916', 'CAMBRAI 1917', and 'FRANCE AND FLANDERS 1914-1918'.

Left: An Indian soldier in lightweight service dress and Pattern 1903 equipment, France c.1915. There was a large number of Indian Army troops sent to the Western Front in 1914, where they fought bravely in the cold and damp conditions of French Flanders. The first Indian troops to arrive in France only came wearing their thin KD uniform, so suffered through most of the winter in 1914 until thicker serge was issued in December 1914. The Corps was transferred to the Middle East at the end of 1915 which was a more suitable theatre of war for Indian troops

Two Indian sepoys pose with RFC men. The Indians are wearing their distinctive 'Pagris' headdress and wearing the 'Kurta' shirt-like blouse. Sikhs continued to wear the turban throughout the war, as they objected so strongly to the wearing of steel helmets that they were never issued to them. The RFC men are wearing the Pattern 1908 'pistol' set with supporting brace attachments.

A Poona Horse officer on the Somme in August 1915, wearing the 'Kurta', the shirt-like blouse common to Indian troops. When the First World War broke out the Poona Horse was stationed at Secunderabad in India as a part of the 9th (Secunderabad) Cavalry Brigade, 2nd Indian Cavalry Division, and were to become the first Indian Cavalry regiment to be engaged in the war. The French gave *Les Hindous*, as they called all Indian troops, an enthusiastic welcome when they landed in France during October 1914.

Two Gurkha riflemen in France, displaying the fearsome 'kukri', which reputedly could sever arms and remove heads in a single blow. The kukri is a broad-bladed, leaf-shaped knife with a single edged heavy twelve-inch curved blade. It was an all-purpose tool, not just a weapon, and used for chopping wood, digging holes, butchering meat and even opening tins. Men from both the Gurkha and Garwhali Rifles wore the slouch hat; the Gurkhas turned the left side up, the Garwhalis the right.

Above: Burmese Labour Corps in France. Over 300,000 foreign laborers were employed by the British to support the men of the Labour Corps. Some of these men were black soldiers from Empire countries like Fiji, Seychelles, Mauritius, Bermuda, British West Indies and Burma, who were used as laborers rather than fighting soldiers.

Below: The Burmese Labour Corps was part of the Indian Labour Corps. The majority of foreign 'native' laborers were civilians from Egypt (100,000), China (100,000), South Africa (20,000) and India (21,000) who were recruited in their own countries and transported to France for a fixed term. This ranged from nine month contracts for the Egyptians to three years for the South Africans. Many of the Burmese agreed to stay on until the war ended rather than being repatriated when their contracts had finished. They are photographed here with Scots from the 1/7th Gordon Highlanders.

Chinese Labour Corps NCOs with a sergeant of the Durham Light Infantry. Note the Chinese wearing pinned on rank chevrons. The man on the right is wearing cloth numbers "C.L.C 33613" which identifies his unit and army number.

A Labour Corps corporal with two Chinese laborers. The laborers contracts meant that they were not to be used within ten miles of the frontlines, so the majority of them were employed at the ports and railheads loading and unloading stores.

Men of the Chinese Labour Corps in France. By the end of the war over a hundred thousand Chinese served in a non-combatant labor role on the Western Front, for both the British and French. They were employed in any labor task from working in the French docks to clearing the battlefield. They were kitted out with blue cotton suits, a flannel shirt, a waistcoat, a pair of woolen drawers, a brown canvas raincoat and standard British ankle boots with puttees.

Chapter Six

Infantry Weapons

A Scottish soldier armed with an early Lee-Metford 303-inch rifle. The Lee-Metford was used from the early 1890's until replaced at the latter end of the century with the charger loading Lee-Enfield Mk.I rifle, or 'long lee'. Metford's were used during the First World War for training purposes.

A West Yorkshire Regiment Other Rank with a No.1 Mark III 303-inch Short, Magazine Lee-Enfield (SMLE) and an early Pattern 1907 'hook quillon' bayonet. The SMLE replaced the older 'long lees' and the shorter cavalry carbines after the Boer War, thus issuing all troops with a universal rifle. The SMLE, introduced in 1907, was five inches shorter and weighed almost a pound less than its predecessor. It had a back sight graduated to 2,000 yards and a ten-round magazine that could be loaded by five-round charger clips.

A soldier armed with a Canadian Ross rifle and bayonet. At the start of the war the CEF's main rifle was the Canadian Pattern 1910 Ross Mark III 303-inch rifle. The Ross was designed more for accurate marksmanship instead of the rigors of trench warfare, which immediately proved problematic. In June 1916 the SMLE had wholly replaced the Ross, however because of its superior accuracy the Ross was still kept on by some Canadian snipers.

A private from the 15th (Civil Service Rifles) Battalion, London Regiment, armed with a Japanese Arisaka Model 38 rifle. The Arisaka rifle, introduced in 1905, was named after Colonel Nariakira Arisaka, who headed a commission during the 1890s that was charged with developing a new rifle for the Japanese. The British purchased the rifle from Japan and used them in training, guard duty and home defense. In 1915 many were sold onto Russia when the SMLE became more widely available. The photograph is dated February 2nd, 1916.

Above: Lancashire Fusiliers sparring with 'sword' bayonets. The Pattern 1907 'sword' bayonet, introduced in 1908, had a single edged 17-inch blade. Early versions had a hooked fighting quillon on the cross-guard, which was dispensed with from 1913.

Below: A Queen's (Royal West Surrey Regiment) Sniper Section in France, armed with No.1 Mark III SMLE's with side mounted telescopic sights. The side mounted scope was introduced in 1915 and designed to aid charger loading. It was over twelve inches long, with a field of view of 9.5 degrees and an eye relief of three inches. The drum was ranged from 100 to 600 yards.

Above: A photograph of a New Zealander sniper, marked on the reverse, "To All from Peter – For old times sake 31/7/16". He is armed with a No.1 Mark III SMLE with a 'Periscopic Prism Co' side-mounted scope. Note the brass marksman badge to his lower left-hand sleeve.

Right: A sergeant sniper laden down in 'trench' gear. This sniper is equipped with prismatic binoculars, a sniper scope in leather case, an emergency ration bag, PH gas hood bag, a rolled 'crawl' suit and has sandbags wrapped around his legs to help keep mud off the puttees.

Above: A sniper section in France with captured German souvenirs, including the prized Pickelhaube. The sniper rifles are equipped with the offset mounted scopes. These were commonly manufactured by the Periscopic Prism Company Ltd., and also Aldis Brothers who became two of the largest suppliers of sniper scopes for the SMLE.

Below: "Some of the scrounging scouts" from the London Scottish, Arras, July 1918. One man is armed with a Pattern 14 rifle, which was popular with snipers because of its excellent accuracy. Also note that the Pattern 1908 pouches are of a peg variety, whilst the Pattern 1914 pouches are the modified version with double straps. Some are wearing MM ribbons and most have the inverted red triangle patch of the 168th Brigade, 56th (London) Division. A Scout section was the pick of a battalion, employed as a kind of intelligence and reconnaissance section. They were trained in map reading, use of the compass and telescope, observation, report writing, setting up observation posts, concealment, use of aerial photos, night movement and patrolling. They worked very closely with the battalion snipers.

1/9th (Queen Victoria's Rifles) Battalion, London Regiment 'bombers', sometimes called 'grenadiers', in a trench wearing grenade waistcoats and holding No.1 grenades c.1915. Each waistcoat carrier had ten grenade pockets and its weight was supported by a neck strap and waist tie-tapes. Note the sacks which probably contain extra bombs. The definition of the term 'bomb' was clarified in January 1916 as a projectile fired from trench howitzers or dropped from an aircraft. A 'grenade' was a projectile thrown by hand or by a machine, or fired from a rifle.

An officer wearing a cuff rank jacket, steel helmet, box respirator and holding a Webley Mk.VI revolver. The six chambered, self-ejecting .455 Webley Service Revolver was one of the most commonly used pistols by the British. As well as being the main sidearm of the officer, it was also used by warrant officers, staff sergeants, dispatch riders and machine-gunners.

Above: A Royal Fusiliers trench raiding party. They are armed with an assortment of revolvers, automatic pistols, trench daggers, rifles, grenades and even a 'Stokes' mortar bomb. Stokes bombs were used on raids for the demolishing of dugouts or emplacements when a larger explosive charge was required. Note all are wearing shorts, with their knees and knuckles bandaged.

Below: Lieutenant Ramsden, 1/8th Battalion (Leeds Rifles), West Yorkshire Regiment with the Battalion Bomber's in 1916. In 1916 grenade throwers officially became known as 'bombers'. The basic bombing party consisted of one NCO, two bayonet men, two throwers, two carriers and two spare men. Note the wearing of the small metal flaming-grenade badges on the left sleeve, instead of the official cloth 'bombers' pattern.

Above: Bomber's wearing the ten-pocket grenade waistcoat that was designed originally for carrying the No.6 and 7 'Lemon' grenades, but was also used extensively for the No.5 'Mills' bomb. Note the adapted water buckets with pull-strings, utilized to carry extra bombs.

Below: Bomber's from the 24th (The Queen's) Battalion, London Regiment in rest billets, France. All are armed with the No.2, Mark II 'Mexican' Grenade. Adopted as a stopgap measure, this grenade was introduced in February 1915 from initial stock held for a Mexican and Brazilian contract by the Cotton Powder Co. The officer is holding a German stick grenade. All men are wearing sack covered first issue steel helmets with two-part chinstraps and have PH bags. They wear brass 'T/24/Londons' shoulder titles, cloth 'QUEENS L.R.' and also the bomber's skill-at-arms badge in the shape of a red flaming bomb, as introduced in 1915. The postcard is dated August 1916.

Above: Royal Fusiliers with SMLE cup dischargers at training school, 1918. The No.1 discharger cup enabled the No.36 'Mills' bomb to reach distances of 200 yards, as opposed to 30 yards if thrown by hand. The wire-bound, reinforced SMLE rifle used as a discharger was often called an 'EY' rifle, reputedly after its inventor, Edward Yule.

Below: A Leicestershire Regiment officer at Bombing School. A selection of the most commonly used grenades, in use by the British Army in 1917 are shown here. They include the No.1, No.2 'Mexican', No.3 'Hales', No.5 'Mills', No.15 'Ball', No.19 and No.20 grenades. There is also a trench mortar (with modified SMLE action), a 'Very' flare pistol and signal rockets.

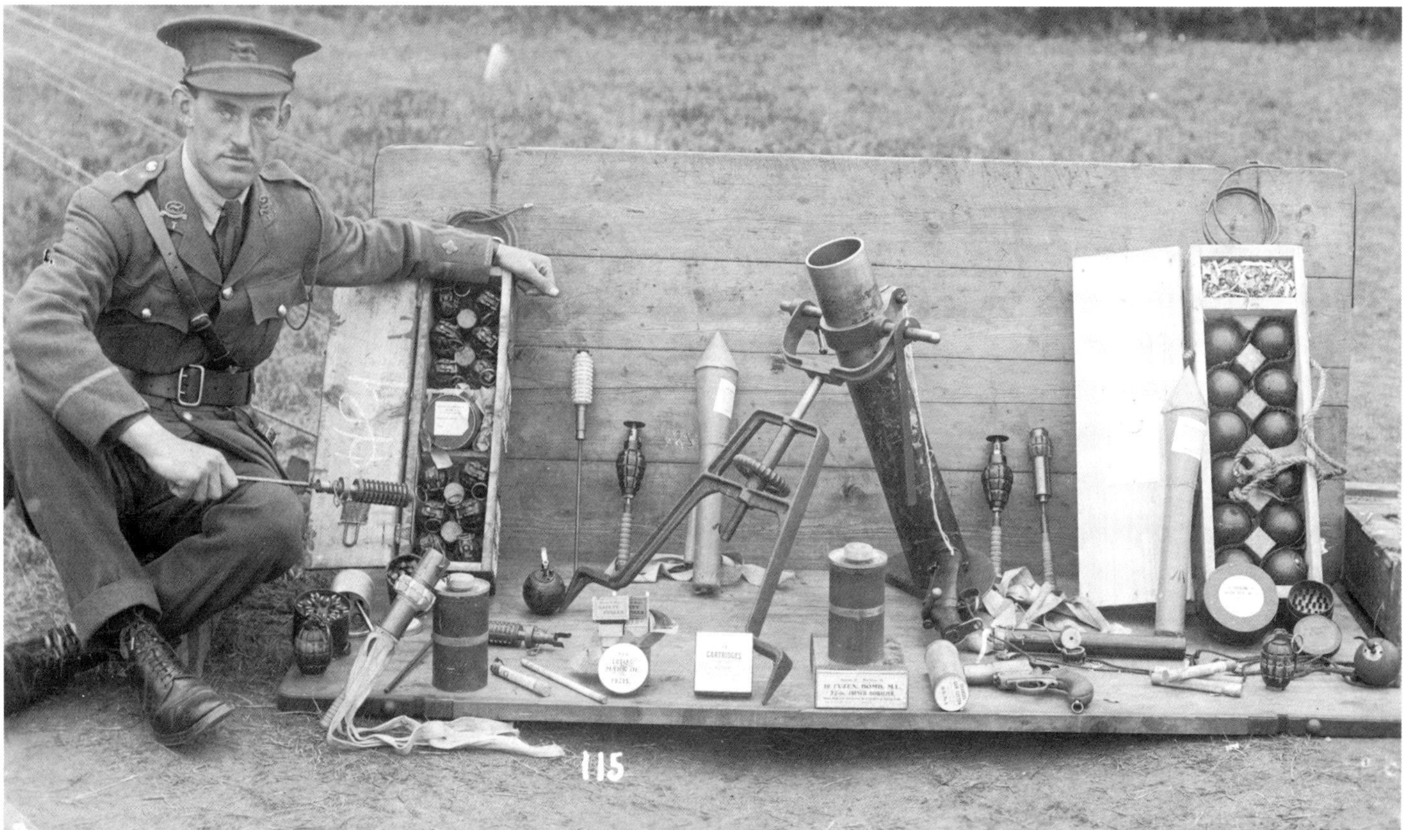

Above: NCO's and officers at bombing school in France, 1917. A display of No.1, No.2 and a sectionalized 'Mills' No.5, along with various rifle grenades can be seen. The Mills came in three variants officially called the No.5, No.23 or No.36 that could be hand thrown or adapted for firing from a rifle. More than 70 million Mills grenades were manufactured from its first appearance in May 1915 to the end of the war.

Below: Army Ordnance Corps NCOs examining a stockpile of ordnance at the end of the war. Still today on the First World War battlefields tons of explosives are unearthed every year, the 'Iron Harvest' as it has come to be known.

Above: A Pattern 1901 303-inch Maxim machine-gun of the Gloucestershire Regiment. In 1914, all infantry battalions were equipped with a machine-gun section of two maxim guns, which in February 1915 was increased to four.

Below: A London Scottish 'MG' section in England, before they landed in France in September 1914. Infantry battalions relinquished responsibility for machine-guns when the Machine Gun Corps (MGC) was formed in October 1915. The London Scottish was amongst the first to be equipped with the Vickers gun.

Above: 1/6th Battalion, Seaforth Highlanders 'MG' section on the Somme in August 1915. Note the MG carts in the background that are marked on the side "6th Seaforth High. 162nd Inf. Brigade, 51st (Highland) Division". Although the British adopted the Vickers in November 1912 thus making the old brass-jacketed Enfield manufactured Maxim obsolete by the start of the First World War, the Maxim remained in service and was still being manufactured in 1917.

Below: Machine Gun Corps (MGC) section in England. Attached to the water jackets are 'Sangster' mounts, a light and more portable version of the heavy Mark IV tripod. A Barr & Stroud Rangefinder and a Sighting Telescope can been seen in the foreground. Shortly after the formation of the MGC in October 1915, the older Maxim guns were replaced by the lighter and improved Pattern 1912 Mark I Vickers, which became the standard heavy machine-gun for the next five decades.

Above: MGC section with their Vickers 'MGs' or 'Emma Gees' as they were commonly known. Note the captured German 08 Maxim on its trench mount. The Vickers machine-gun is cooled by water held in a jacket against the barrel. The gun weighed 28.5 pounds, the water another 10. The tripod weighed 20 pounds. Bullets were assembled into a canvas belt, which held 250-rounds, which would last 30 seconds at the maximum rate of fire of 500 rounds per minute.

Below: Northumberland Fusiliers wearing the Pattern 1908 Lewis Magazine Equipment, as introduced in 1917. Four pouches, each containing two 47-round magazines, were worn strapped together. With a rate of fire up to 700 rounds per minute, in short bursts, a magazine could be used up in a little over four seconds.

A Canadian Lewis Gunner armed with a .455-inch Webley service revolver and a Lewis 303-inch machinegun. He is wearing an SD cap, jacket with leather football buttons and the machine-gunners style Pattern 1908 equipment. This set comprised of a web belt, shoulder straps and a leather holster and ammunition pouch. He wears other ranks mounted pattern 'trench' boots with a pair of heavily repaired breeches. The Lewis had a 47-round pan magazine, fully automatic and was light and mobile enough in comparison to the Vickers to keep up with and support the infantry in an advance.

Above: Canadian Lewis gunners. The Lewis was a shoulder-controlled air-cooled light automatic weapon, weighing 26 pounds. The weapon was carried and fired by one man, but he needed another man to carry and load the magazines. Lewis guns were supplied to the army from July 1915, initially the official establishment was four per infantry battalion (and per cavalry regiment), but by July 1918, infantry battalions possessed 36 each, and even the pioneer battalions had twelve.

Below: 1/7th Battalion (Leeds Rifles), West Yorkshire Regiment with their Lewis guns in 1916. The men at the front wear the 'MG' skill-at-arms badge, at this date the 'LG' Lewis Gunner badge had not been authorized. When the MGC was created in 1915 to provide a machine-gun company per brigade, the Vickers/Maxim guns were withdrawn; replacing the infantry at battalion level with the lighter Lewis gun, nicknamed the 'Belgian Rattlesnake'.

A Canadian machine-gun section with tripod mounted gas-operated Model 1895/14 Colt-Browning machine-guns. This was the first successful gas operated machine-gun, from a basic design by American John Moses Browning. The first Colt was nicknamed the 'Potato Digger', derived from the fact that there is a very heavy operating lever below the barrel that swings in a half arc. If the tripod is set too low, or the earth happens to be soft at the point of mounting, under progressive fire the tripod burrows in and the operating lever will churn up the ground.

The 6th Brigade Trench Mortar Battery with a French interpreter and 'Stokes' mortars. By May 1916 it was decided to standardize on three types of mortar: the 3-inch (light) 'Stokes', the 2-inch (medium) 'Toffee Apple' (superseded in June 1917 by the 6-inch Newton Mortar), and by the end of 1916 the 9.45-inch (heavy) 'Flying Pig'.

Manchester men from the 127th Brigade Trench Mortar Battery, France 1917. Wilfred Stokes invented the Stokes 3-inch mortar in 1915; it was a design of brilliant simplicity, which became standard issue in the army for several decades. In March 1916, the medium trench mortar batteries formally came under the command of divisional artillery, whilst the light Stokes batteries, left at battalion level control, came under brigade command. At this time, each division was given a Divisional Trench Mortar Officer, the batteries were numbered, and a skill-at-arms badge, in the shape of a blue flaming bomb, was introduced to identify mortar personnel.

A Royal Engineer Special 'Gas' Brigade Trench Mortar Battery with an officer from the Somerset Light Infantry. The 4-inch Stokes came into service in 1916, and was generally used for projecting gas bombs, both lethal and lachrymatory.

A Somerset Light Infantry officer with a Royal Engineers 4-inch Stokes Trench Mortar Battery, France 1918. The 5th Battalion, Special 'Gas' Brigade, RE operated the 4-inch Stokes used for projecting gas. Each projectile contained two litres of liquid gas, nearly three times as much as in a 6-inch howitzer shell. Concentration of gas could be applied to a target by rapid fire. It was claimed that a well-trained mortar crew could get 15 bombs in the air before the first one had struck its target.

X/20 and Y/20 Batteries (20th Light Division) Trench Mortar Brigade, RFA, France 1918. The 6-inch 'Newton' Mortar superseded the 2-inch 'Toffee Apple' mortar in June 1917. The Newton rested on a steel base plate and was held by three adjustable support lines of steel wire. The weapon fired a 48 lb. finned bomb, with a simple percussion fuse in the nose, to a range of about 800 yards.

15th (Scottish) Division Trench Mortar Battery in France, 1918. Their 6-inch 'Newton' is mounted on a wheeled carriage to aid transport. Note the 48 lb. finned mortar bomb. The Newton remained in service, admittedly in a reserve role, until the early years of World War II.

RAMC medics wearing Hypo 'smoke' helmets, in almost certainly a posed photograph. Note the 'casualty' wearing the early 'Black Veiling' respirator with its pad and 4-inch veil to cover the eyes. Since the use of gas in April 1915 a variety of anti-gas protection was used. Initially only a pad tied around the mouth and nose, but by the summer of 1915 the 'H' (Hypo) smoke helmet was issued. This flannel bag with a single celluloid window was dipped in a soda solution and kept moist by treatment with glycerin.

An RE corporal with a Hypo bag carried over his shoulder and what appears to be either a 'Black Veiling' respirator or tear gas-goggle bag attached to his chest pocket. The photograph dates from September 1915.

A bombardier wearing a Phenate-Hexamine (PH) tube helmet. The Phenate 'P' helmet was introduced in December 1915, and consisted of a chemical impregnated flannel cloth with two glass eyepieces and a mouth exhalation valve. Both the 'H' and 'P' helmets were good enough to combat the affects of chlorine, but not phosgene gas which was introduced in January 1916. The 'PH' helmet was introduced to help combat phosgene, and stayed in use until 1917.

Left: A Seaforth Highlander CSM with medals ribbons for the DCM and Boer War campaign. He is wearing a 'PH' helmet, correctly worn tucked into the collar. Breath was drawn through the chemically impregnated cloth, and exhaled through the mouth valve. The helmet was obviously discomforting and it severely limited a soldier's ability to see and hear, let alone shoot accurately.

Opposite
A YMCA officer with his spoils of war – a collectors delight with everything from early gas masks to the leather British tank helmet.

Above: Officers from the 2nd Battalion, Lancashire Fusiliers pose wearing 'PH' gas hoods. The 'PH' was not proof against all gases, and was displaced from August 1916 onwards by the small box respirator. The 'PH' remained in use until 1917, when it was slightly modified into the 'PHG' helmet, which had the addition of permanently attached goggles.

Below: Officers with small box respirators at the ready. The box respirator was trialed as early as February 1916 by the Royal Engineers, but it was not until the latter half of 1916 that they were issued to the troops. The mask, seen here being worn, was an unwieldy design but gave far better protection against the different gases than the earlier hood patterns.

Above: The Small Box Respirator or 'SBR' as introduced in the latter half of 1916. The box respirator design was adopted by the United States as well as many other countries, and used throughout the Second World War. The respirator was ordered to be carried within three miles of the front line.

Below: Australian machine-gunners from the 43rd Battalion, AIF in France. They carry box respirators and tear gas rubber-sponge goggles at the ready. Gas goggles were carried by all troops in addition to the SBR in case of a Lachrymatory or tear gas attack. The photograph is dated April 3rd, 1918

Chapter Seven

MGC and Tank Corps

MGC infantry wearing Pattern 1914 on a mixture of 1902 SD and khaki fatigue dress. The experience of fighting to date had proved that machine-guns required special tactics and organization, which led to the creation of the Machine Gun Corps. The MGC consisted of infantry machine-gun companies, cavalry machine-gun squadrons, and motor machine-gun batteries.

The 96th MGC Company (32nd Division) on the Somme 1916. They are armed with Vickers 303-inch machine-guns with additional 'Sangster' mounts, a smaller version of the tripod, strapped under the water jacket. These were used to increase mobility, but disappeared from service by the close of the war.

No.1 Section, 'A' Company, 8th Battalion MGC, in France. Note the limbers with the 8th Divisional emblem of a large four-sided white square incorporating a smaller four-sided red square.

MGC officers with machine-gun limbers. On the reverse it says "With the mules in France".

A group of MGC officers in France. Note the officer at the back still wears Royal Sussex collar insignia of his former regiment, although wearing a MGC badged field service cap. Officers wore regimental insignia of their regiment until officially gazetted into their new units.

Right: MGC officers, a major in a cuff rank and a lieutenant in a shoulder rank 'wind-up' jacket. Note the cloth MGC company insignia to the arms, and the majors Military Cross ribbon. The photograph is dated May 6th, 1918.

Below right: Two Northumberland brothers. One is from a Northumberland Fusiliers pioneer battalion, whilst his brother has recently been transferred to the MGC, although he still wears the buttons and shoulder title of the Northumberland Fusiliers. Reverse is dated August 16th, 1917.

Below: A Scottish MGC officer from the 51st (Highland) Division, wearing the MGC badge on his Tam-o'-Shanter. Scottish officers and men refused to adopt the service dress cap in this division after the creation of the MGC.

MGC men from the 4th Division wearing Pattern 1908 'pistol kit'. Note the shoulder braces are folded back onto themselves in order to provide support for the revolver holster and ammunition pouch, a more commonly used configuration than the specialist brace attachments.

Above: A MGC private wearing the specialist Pattern 1908 brace attachments. Introduced in 1913 they were originally designed for pipers and rangefinders, and used during the war by the RFC and the MGC. The pistol is a .455-inch Webley service revolver, worn with two leather ammunition pouches.

Right: Machine gunners from what appears to be the 24th Division in France c.1916. They all wear Pattern 1902 SD jackets with drab serge shorts and Pattern 1914 'pistol' equipment. Note the divisional insignia on the arms and also the four-piece issued helmet cover of the man on the left.

Above: No.4 Section, 2nd (Life Guards) Machine Gun Battalion at Wivelghem, Belgium in December 1918. Note the Pattern 1908 brace attachments and leather pistol pouches being worn.

A 7th (Cyclist) Battalion, Welsh Regiment Hotchkiss machine-gunner wearing the leather Hotchkiss pattern bandolier. The cavalry's principle machine-gun was the Hotchkiss Mark I 303-inch Machine Gun, the replacement for the Maxim machine-guns withdrawn to help equip the MGC. The Hotchkiss came into service with the cavalry in 1916, and remained in service until declared obsolete in 1946.

A MGC Scottish corporal, 51st Battalion MGC in a badged Tam-o'-Shanter, leather football style buttoned jacket and Military Medal ribbon. Machine-gunners of the 51st continued to wear Scottish headdress after the creation of the MGC, refusing to adopt the service dress cap.

Right: A gunner from a Motor Machine Gun section. Note the MMG cap badge and cloth sign with a 'RFA' (Royal Field Artillery) shoulder title. Many of the MMG joined from RFA batteries, and were later seconded into the Tank Corps.

Below: A Tank Corps private wearing the white-on-khaki worsted 'TC' title and an embroidered tank badge, as sanctioned in May 1917 for all those who had passed the tank training course. Initially called the Heavy Section, Machine Gun Corps, they became the Tank Corps at the end of July 1917.

Below right: A Tank Corps private wearing the white-on-khaki worsted 'TC' and specialist tank sleeve badge. The black and white checked tally is the insignia of the Tank Salvage Unit, c.1918.

"Yours to a Cinder Wally, France 1918". A Tank Corps man wearing a cloth tank badge with metal 'Tanks' shoulder title insignia. Cloth battle flashes were also worn to distinguish the tank company or battalion.

A Tank Corps corporal wearing a Military Medal and Bar. Note the four wound stripes on his left sleeve. Army Order 249, of July 6th, 1916, saw the introduction of the wound stripe, approved for officers and men wounded on or after August 4th, 1914.

'G' Battalion, Tank Corps private in Pattern 1914 pistol order. Note the colored slip-on shoulder tallies that denote the tank battalion. These were introduced to identify tank battalions in January 1917. 'G' Battalion wore halved green and red cloth slip-ons.

Left: A Tank Corps man wearing a MGC cap badge. The Tank Corps did not have a badge of its own until July 1917. The tank sleeve badge was issued under General Routine Order of May 7th, 1917 and presented upon completion of tank training.

Opposite
Top: 6th Battalion, Tank Corp crew in France. The Heavy Section, MGC became officially known as the Tank Corps on July 28th, 1917. The Tank Corps became the Royal Tank Corps in October 1923, a long overdue honor that had been earned many times over during the Great War.

Bottom: A humorous group photograph of Heavy Section, Machine Gun Corps men wearing an incongruous mix of headdress. Note the man seated is wearing the leather tank man's crash helmet, issued in 1916 to help prevent concussion inside a tank. The pattern of headdress was withdrawn the following year as it was thought to resemble the German helmet. A Mark I tank is just visible in the background.

On the reverse is written "Somme, 1918". A 28-ton Mark IV Male Tank with her crew of one officer and eight men. This was the most common variant of the tank, entering service in May 1917. The male tanks had 6-pounder guns, whilst the females were armed with machine-gun only.

A 14-ton 'Whippet' Tank. The Whippet was at first known as the 'Triton Chaser' after its designer, Sir William Triton, but later officially named 'Tank, Medium Mark A'. These were relatively light and were equipped with three machine-guns, and being capable of speeds up to eight miles per hour, was the fastest tank the British Army possessed.

Chapter Eight

Royal Artillery

Two Territorial London Brigade RFA gunners photographed by a gun limber in England. They are part of the 47th (London) Division that departed to France in March 1915. They wear Pattern 1903 haversacks and water bottles.

Above: Territorial Royal Field Artillery NCO's with their officer in England. This photograph is probably pre-war as the officer wears twisted drab cord shoulder straps that were introduced in 1904, and worn until 1913 when replaced with sewn down cloth shoulder straps.

Below: 87th Siege Battery Signal Section, Royal Garrison Artillery. They display signaling flags and tripod mounted Heliographs. The Heliograph was an apparatus used by the British Army for signaling by flashes of light.

Above: A studio portrait of a Royal Artillery bombardier wearing the 'L' trade badge for a gun layer. He also wears a Pattern 1905 SD cap with thin brown leather chin strap and a khaki drill cover with neck-flap.

Above right: A nicely composed studio photograph of an artillery Company Sergeant Major, denoted by the brass crown with gun above the rank chevrons. The large cloth unit patch is unidentified. The photograph is dated 1918.

Right: A studio portrait of a gunner wearing a 'RFA' cloth title on the arm. This pattern of cloth title was originally issued as slip-on titles for the shoulder straps to wear in place of metal titles, but many units chose to sew them directly onto the jacket. Note the white lanyard worn around the left shoulder.

Above left: A studio portrait of Bombardier Grimshaw, RFA. In Italy, Egypt and Mesopotamia the drab serge service dress was issued alongside the khaki drill uniform, and commonly worn with the Wolseley Pattern helmet. Note the Territorial Force Proficiency Star on the sleeve.

Above: A Bombardier in shirt-sleeve order, c.1915. This photograph shows details of the pattern of pantaloon worn by the mounted services, with slanted pockets, padded seat insert, leather inside leg reinforcement and tin buttons. The original paper label that would bear the manufacturers name, size and date is also just visible. On his braces he wears the single red identity disk as introduced in August 1914.

Left: A studio photograph taken in France of two RFA bombardiers in leather jerkins. The jerkin was an intended replacement for the animal skin coats that were worn through the early winters of the war. The jerkin, offering protection from the cold and rain, had a warm blanket lining and fastened by plain leather buttons.

Opposite
An artillery sergeant wearing a simplified jacket over a leather jerkin, which is just visible protruding from the bottom of his jacket. He is equipped with Pattern 1903 pistol kit with a bandolier and binocular case. Note the riding boots worn over his puttees.

Opposite
Left: A fine photograph of Private J. King, Royal Artillery, wearing Pattern 1903 pistol kit. This comprised of a 1903 belt to which was attached a pistol holster and an ammunition pouch. Dated on the reverse "Xmas 1917".

Top right: "Just out of the line". Note the thigh length long rubber waders or 'gum' boots and the shorter length 'Wellington' style boots. Both patterns were winter issue to troops in the line from trench stores. The photograph is dated March 12th, 1916.

Bottom right: An artillery signaler in an animal skin jacket, a SD soft cap and trench boots, winter 1916. The jackets, commonly made of goat or sheepskins, were popularly nicknamed 'teddy bears', 'wooly bears and 'stinkers'.

A classic field photograph of an artillery man in a winter 'teddy bear' coat. He is lightly equipped with a Pattern 1903 leather bandolier and PH bag. He wears the service dress soft cap that was introduced during the autumn of 1916.

Gunner G. Manton, Guards Division Trench Mortar Battery, in a white animal skin jacket. Note the large ding in his steel helmet.

Above: A photograph of a driver, dated December 2nd, 1916. He wears a long sleeve black goatskin jacket, leather gauntlet gloves with holster and ammunition pouch. Note the Royal Artillery cap badge attached to the sacking helmet cover.

Above right: An artilleryman in France, winter 1916/1917. He wears a wet, mud splattered leather jerkin, Pattern 1903 bandolier and PH bag. He is photographed in an outside studio with painted backdrop and flowerpot stand, common features in so many active service 'carte postale' photographs. Note the snow on the ground.

Right: A gunner wearing the other ranks pattern of leather 'trench' boot, almost identical to that worn by the officer. These were commonly lace-up with a three-buckle closure at the top He also wears the early War Office pattern of steel helmet, distinguishable by the two-piece leather chinstrap and raw edge.

An artilleryman wearing a sacking covered helmet affixed with a cap badge. Note the two overseas stripes and the two long service good conduct chevrons that denote six years service. Overseas stripes were introduced in January 1918 (Army Orders 4 and 20 of 1918) and worn on the lower right arm to denote service overseas during the First World War. The number of stripes indicated the number of years served overseas from 1914.

Royal Artillery bombardier photographed in a popular Arras location. He is equipped with the Pattern 1903 bandolier, a haversack and also a small box respirator, c.1917.

Above: Photographed in Arras, these Royal Artillery officers are all wearing private purchased helmet covers, as retailed through popular outfitters like 'Hawkes & Co' and 'Woodrow of Piccadilly'. Note that one also wears the ribbon on the Military Cross.

Above right: "Three Trench Mortar Merchants in war paint (very fierce)" photographed at Bully-Grenay, near Lens in September 1918. The officers from the X/23 Trench Mortar Battery are wearing the two different variations of the box respirator satchel, with mounted and dismounted carry-strap configurations.

Right: Artillery officers wearing light colored winter service Gor'blimey caps. Light shaded caps, shirts, ties and breeches became very popular with officers during the early part of the war until darker drab colors became the approved shade for service dress.

A group of Territorial RFA gunners photographed at Le Brebis, July 29th, 1916. They wear a mix of field modified Gor'blimey caps without the fold-down piece and Pattern 1905 SD caps. The man seated, second from the left wears a drab serge SD soft cap, approved in March 1916 and issued during autumn of that year.

A group from 7th Battery, RFA (7th Division) in rest billets at Bouzincourt, on the Somme, 1916. Most wear the Gor'blimey winter cap, with or without the cover, and others the de-stiffened 1905 SD caps. The Gor'blimey cap was popular wear with the artillery.

"Somewhere in France 1917", a popular caption due to wartime censorship. The gunners are all wearing winter animal skin coats, both sleeved and un-sleeved, with steel 'shrapnel' helmets.

Opposite
Top: Photographed close to the line by a sandbagged ammunition dump. Notice the wooden 18-pdr shell packing boxes on the left. They all wear Pattern 1902 service dress with steel helmets.

Bottom left: Two gunnery sergeants in Italy. One has a Gor'blimey which has been modified slightly by the removal of the fold-down piece. The other man has a SD soft cap as introduced during the autumn of 1916.

Bottom right: An artillery driver in a double-breasted, mounted pattern greatcoat. He wears a Gor'blimey, leather driver's gauntlets, Pattern 1903 9-pocket bandolier and is armed with a No.1 Mk.III SMLE rifle. Artillery drivers rode the horse teams, which pulled the guns and ammunition limbers.

I HEAR
YOU
CALLING ME

Opposite
Top left: An artilleryman wearing a fur lined mounted pattern greatcoat and Gor'blimey. He is posing with a sailor from H.M.S *Benbow*, who wears the canvas uniform of the Royal Navy. The photograph is dated January 1st, 1917.

Top right: An artillery driver in the standard mounted pattern greatcoat. Attached to his service dress cap is a pair of early pattern rubber goggles, first issued to the Royal Flying Corps before the war as flying kit.

Bottom left: An artilleryman with a pair of Model 'D' field telephones, as introduced before the war. Photographed in Gallipoli during 1915, this image shows the lack of service dress often worn there during the sweltering summer months. Note the sleeveless flannel shirt, worn breeches and crushed SD cap.

Bottom right: "I hear you calling me" Gunner E. Cresey, Royal Field Artillery poses with the standard Model 'D', Mark III portable buzzing telephone. It comprised of a handset with presser switch to operate the microphone, a small buzzer for calling and signaling with a Morse key, dry batteries and line terminals all enclosed in a metal/leather case.

"What did you do in the Great War, Daddy?" A Royal Horse Artillery gunner with blanket and haversack poses with a uniformed boy. As a patriotic statement during the Great War you could purchase a child's version of a British army or navy uniform.

115th Anti Aircraft Section, Royal Artillery, with a mounted AA gun on a Peerless truck. When it became apparent that productions of Motor Lorries by British manufacturers were being overwhelmed by demand, the War Office seeked additional vehicles from overseas, many coming from the USA, like the Peerless, whilst others came from France, Italy and Switzerland.

18-pdr gun and crew. Regular artillery batteries were completely reissued with new quick-firing (QF) guns of the 13-pdr (RHA) and 18-pdr (RFA) types between 1906 and 1914. The QF gun was not only quick, but also very accurate as it confined the gun's recoil hydraulically to its barrel, thus eliminating the need to run up and re-lay the gun after each shot. Both fired shrapnel only, although the fuse could be set so that a shell would penetrate defenses before bursting.

The 18-pounder QF field gun fired a shell that was 3.3-inch caliber (84mm) and weighed 18.5lbs. It had a maximum range of about 6,500 yards with this distance being covered in a little over 12 seconds. The gun could elevate to 16 degrees above horizontal, which meant that its shell had a fairly flat trajectory. This design proved to be an excellent gun, and was employed by the British Army as their main field artillery piece. With a good crew and conditions, this gun could fire an incredible 30 rounds a minute, over an extended range of 9,300 yards. The gun weighed 2,821 pounds (1.3 tons).

The 6-inch howitzer fired a shell of 6-inch caliber, weighing 118lbs. The gun barrel and breech weighed 30-cwt (approx. 1.5 tons), and had a range of 5,200 yards. The maximum barrel elevation was 35 degrees, which made it less effective for plunging fire against entrenched positions. A new 26-cwt version was produced in 1915 to overcome the range and elevation problem, which raised them to 11,400 yards and 45 degrees respectively. This plus other minor changes considerably improved the usefulness of the weapon, and more than 3,600 saw service in the Great War. One source says they fired more than 22 million rounds. This howitzer weighed 8,142lb (3.7 tons).

The 8-inch Mk.VI howitzer was the power behind the Somme barrage. This howitzer had a range of 10,000 yards, and weighed 9 tons.

'Kanopit' 60-pounder gun. Introduced in 1904 as one of the spate of new specifications issued following the experience of the Boer War, by 1914 it was the mainstay of the RGA's weaponry of the BEF. The shell fired by this gun was 5-inch caliber (127mm) and weighed 60-lb (27.3kg). It had a maximum range of 12,300 yards (11.2km), with this distance being covered in about 16 seconds. Weighing 9,856-lb (4.4 tonnes), the gun was hauled by horses; until modifications were made to facilitate faster manufacture added another ton. This was beyond horse capacity, so it was modified to be pulled by the caterpillar steam tractor.

A British Mark VII naval gun in a camouflaged paint, as use by 29th Siege Battery, RGA.

The 'Persuader' 9.2-inch howitzer, shown here after capture by the Germans during the Spring Offensive in 1918. A brand new development that had only been in production since July 1914, one of these large howitzers went to France with the original BEF, seeing action at Neuve Chapelle in March 1915. The Mk.I howitzer could fire a 290-lb shell 10,000 yards. The howitzer was a sizeable piece of engineering: the three sections of the whole weighed 15.5 tons in total. When being positioned, a box containing a further 9 tons of earth had to be bolted onto the front of the gun platform, to stop a natural tendency to jump (a consequence of a rather short barrel) – this was not a piece designed for rapid movement!

Chapter Nine

Wheels and Transport

The 10th Battalion Queen's (Royal West Surrey Regiment) Horse Transport; one Maltese cart for the Medical Officer, one medical forage cart, four field cookers (one for each company), two water-tank carts and a total of twenty forage carts for general battalion baggage and machine-guns.

Opposite
Top: A General Service (GS) wagon was one of the most common forms of horse drawn transport in use by the British Army. Note the sign 'HORSE T', for Horse Transport and the gold horseshoe divisional sign of the 37th Division.

Bottom: A GS wagon in Albert, Somme, during the summer of 1915. During this period each infantry battalion had a first line of transport that accompanied them, that included three limbered GS wagons to carry tools, e.g. shovels, pickaxes and saws. A further four GS wagons for each battalion were assigned to carry other baggage, stores and supplies.

Above: Private Stanley Brown with a two-horse drawn 'Cart, Water Tank' used by the Kent Brigade, ASC at Deal, England. The photograph is dated September 14th, 1914.

Left: A close up of a Medical General Service Wagon with a painted Geneva Red Cross RAMC sign. This cart carried the battalion's medical supplies.

Opposite
Top: The one-horse drawn Maltese Cart as assigned to the Medical Officer of each battalion in 1915. Note the veil above the horse's eyes, worn to help fend off the flies.

Bottom: A Mk.I Light Ambulance Wagon. To the left of the photograph is the Special Mark I carriage pattern of stretcher fitted with a collapsible hood, useful in hot climates for shielding the patient from the sun and in wet weather for protection from the rain.

A Mk.V Ambulance Wagon with RAMC personnel in a pre-war exercise c.1914. There were two other basic patterns of horse-drawn ambulance wagon, the Mark VI and Mark I (Light).

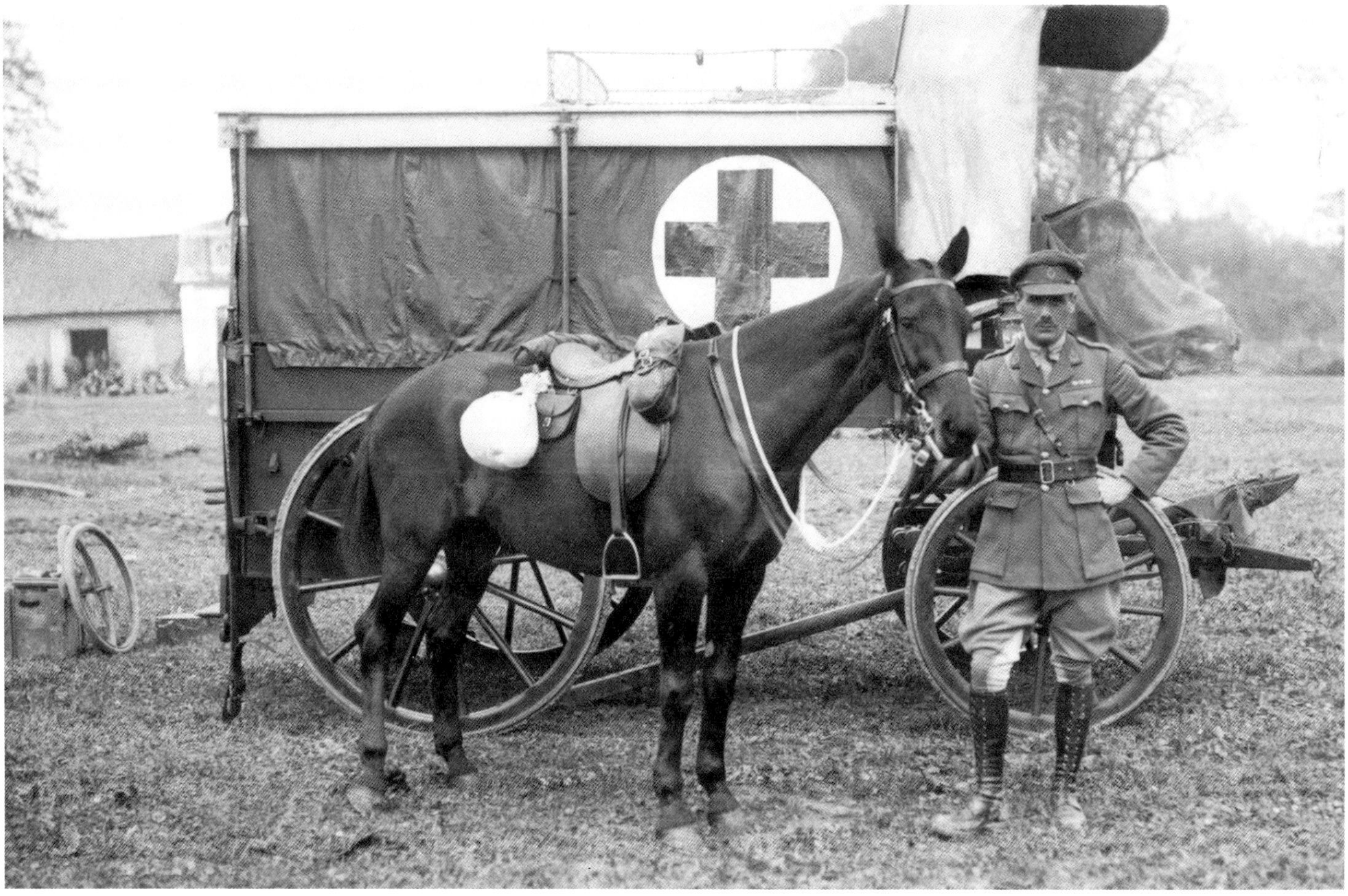

The Commanding Officer of the 54th Field Ambulance (18th Division) stands with his mount by a horsedrawn Mk.VI Ambulance Wagon.

A motorized Ford Model-T Field Ambulance in France with a driver and medic of the RAMC. Note the sandbag covered helmet with RAMC painted badge to the front. Drivers of these vehicles took enormous risks to get the wounded away from the front.

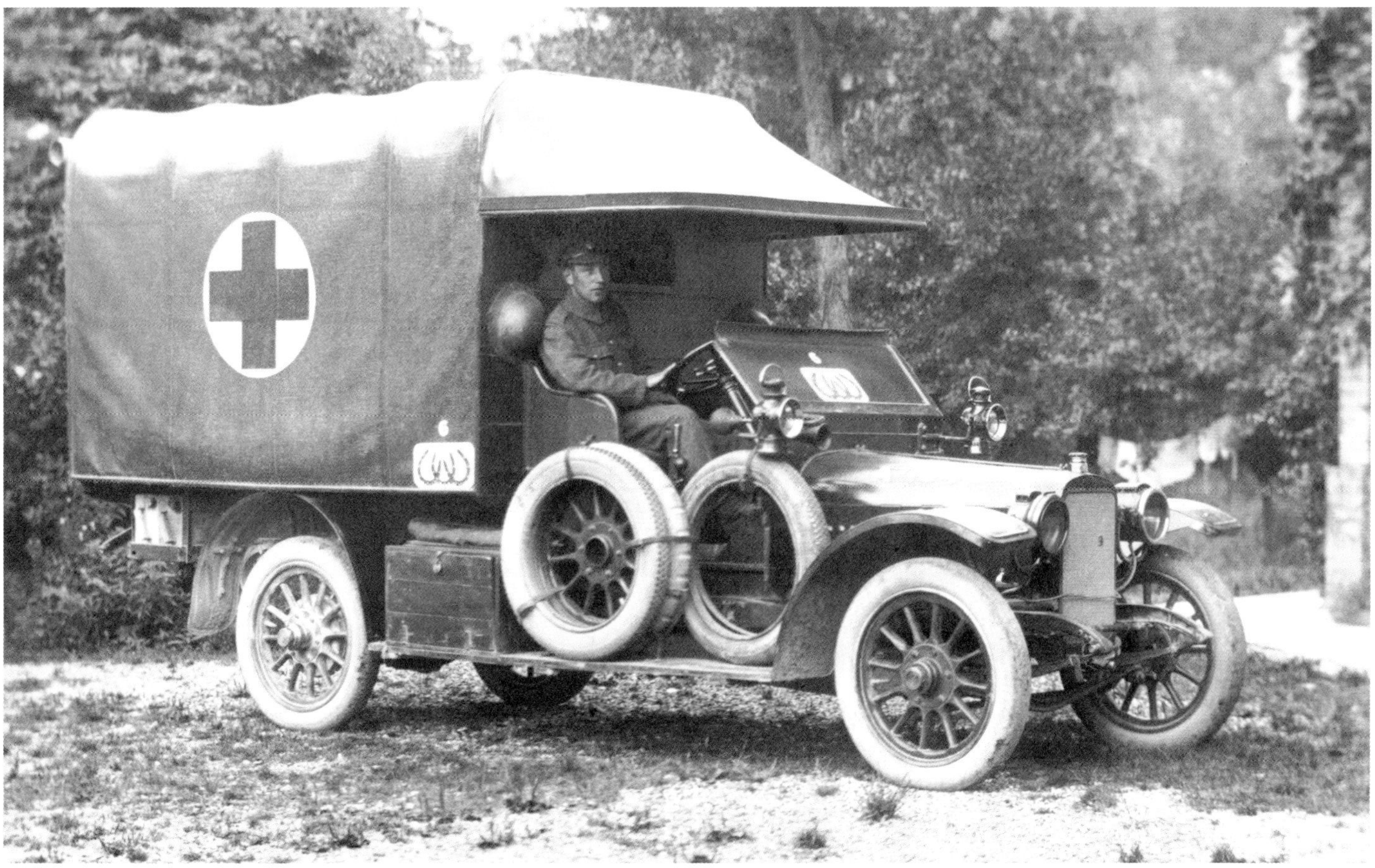

A motorized Field Ambulance with a painted sign of the 3rd Cavalry Division. The Division was formed in October 1914 and saw the war through on the Western Front.

15th (London Welsh) Royal Welsh Fusiliers motorized battalion ambulance. The photograph is dated December 1915, the month the battalion landed in France.

A 28th Divisional Signals Company, Royal Engineers Lorry, in France c.1915. Note the divisional signals XXVIII markings on the side of the vehicle.

A US manufactured Peerless Lorry. The Peerless was supplied to the British Army, along with other U.S. makes like Packard, FWD and Pierce-Arrow. Some 19,360 Lorries were imported for service during 1914-1918 from the USA.

A Thornycroft Lorry attached to 260th Siege Battery, RGA. The Model 'J-type' 4.5-ton lorry was powered by a 30-hp wide valve engine. Over 5000 were supplied to the government during the 1914-1918 war.

A Thornycroft used by the AIF. Private A.F. Gillies poses by his Lorry, photographed on March 29th, 1915 in France. On the back it says "this is a sample of the cars that we brought with us from Australia".

Opposite
Top: A Leyland truck in the services of the RAF. Lorry production increased dramatically during the war, but never did quite fulfill the War Office demands. The most common manufacturers of the standard British Army three-ton Lorry, or 'Y-type', were A.E.C, Dennis and Leyland.

Bottom: 6th Battalion, Seaforth Highlanders by repainted khaki Omnibuses with boarded up windows, probably the 'B-type' 1910 version. Up to early 1915 it was not uncommon to see double-decker London General Omnibuses in their standard livery and blazoned with commercial adverts, commandeered by the ASC's Auxiliary Omnibus Company to transport troops at home and in France and Flanders. This photograph is dated September 1915.

28124
STOW
RA

A 3rd Cavalry Division staff car. Note the divisional sign of the three horseshoes. The Division was formed in October 1914 and saw service throughout the war on the Western Front.

A staff car driven by Sergeant G. Grieves, Anti-Aircraft Section, France 1918.

A car used by YMCA staff in France.

An RE Signals car. On the back of the photograph it says "Somewhere in France on the Amiens/Albert Road, 3/8/15 – 2/Lt H.B. Blower, RE".

A Royal Naval Air Service (RNAS) car, lightly armored in France, probably late 1914. The coats are the short mounted pattern, which one man has supplemented by a long black leather coat.

A Rolls-Royce RNAS Armored Car, armed with a 303-inch Maxim, c.1914. The RNAS Armoured Car Division served in France and Flanders from 1914, Gallipoli in 1915 and the Middle East from 1916.

An American manufactured 75-hp Holt Caterpillar Steam Tractor. These were used to transport large artillery pieces that were beyond the power of horse teams, in particular the 60-pounder and larger howitzers.

A British Army Steam Engine called "Sapper Street'" based behind the lines at Hersin, France. The manufacturing plate shows it as a WD version built by the Hunslet Engineering Company, Leeds in 1917.

Above: "H.J. Perry, France 1917" on a 550cc Triumph Model 'H'. He is wearing a pair of rubber trench waders, a rubberized dispatch riders coat and a leather helmet with goggles. Around his neck is a spare rubber inner tube in case of puncture. Note the Imperial German S98 bayonet complete with frog behind the driving light. He is additionally equipped with a steel helmet, dispatch case, map case, binoculars and a Pattern 1903 leather belt with ammunition pouch and Webley holster.

Opposite
Top: A dispatch rider in France on his Triumph Model 'H' motorbike. Some 30,000 Triumphs were supplied to the British Army from 1915 to 1918. With dispatch riding at their primary function, the 550cc engine, three-speed gearbox with belt drive to the near wheel could achieve a top speed of 45 mph.

Bottom: A Royal Engineer dispatch rider wearing the full dispatch riders rubberized jacket and trouser suit. This pattern of suit was also issued to Lorry drivers who spent many hours in open cabins, exposed to the elements.

Above: 2nd (Life Guards) Machine Gun Section dispatch rider in France in 1918. He wears a rubberized coat and Pattern 1908 pistol set. Note the double strap Pattern 1914 ammunition pouch attached to the Triumph's fuel tank.

Below: An Army Service Corps dispatch rider on a Triumph motorbike marked with the clear and easily recognizable sign of the Guards Division 'ever-open eye'.

Above: A motorcycle rider from the Duke of Wellington's (West Riding Regiment) on a New Hudson model motorbike. Other popular makes were BSA, Triumph, Douglas and Zenith.

Below: An RE Signal Section dispatch rider on a Triumph, with a signalers white over blue brassard with the divisional emblem of the 15th (Scottish) Division, France, c.1918.

A London Territorial RAMC motorcyclist on a Douglas 2.75 hp (348cc) model motorbike, 1918. Some 25,000 models of this kind were supplied to the British Army between 1915 and 1918.

Two of the most popular British Army motorbikes, a BSA and Triumph, side by side.

A Zenith manufactured motorbike. The photograph is dated April 1915 on the reverse.

The 4th Tank Brigade Signal Company, photographed at Basseux near Arras in 1918. Notice the bike with sidecar combination.

A group of dispatch riders from an RE Signals Section, "Somewhere in France". Note the steel helmets and the rider with tear-gas goggles on his Triumph Motorbike handlebars.

Above: Motor Machine Gun Battery using Vickers-Clyno model 5-6hp motorcycle combination. Note the bullet splashed armored shield in front of the Vickers 303-inch machine-gun. By 1918 there were some 1,800 Vickers-Clyno combinations in service.

Below: A RFC motorcyclist and sidecar, marked on the reverse "Poperinge 21-5-17". The 29th Squadron, RFC was based at the Poperinghe aerodrome during most of the war.

"Somewhere in France" RFC dispatch riders. The RFC stayed in regular contact with Army HQ and their gun batteries, where motorcycles provided a means of communication when wired telephone links were unavailable.

A cyclist from the 25th (Cyclist) Battalion, London Regiment. He wears the pattern of leather equipment that was unique to this unit. Note the 'long lee' and equipment attached to the frame of his BSA bicycle, c.1914.

Cyclist F.C. Smith, 6th Platoon, Kent Cyclist Battalion. The unit was deployed for Home defense when war broke out in August 1914.

A Rifle Brigade cyclist in France c.1916. Each infantry battalion had nine bicycles allocated for use by the battalion signalers.

A humorous pose by a 'requisitioned' children's bicycle. Dated on reverse April 24th, 1916.

A line-up of No.3 Section, 'A' Company, 6th (Cyclist) Battalion, Suffolk Regiment in October 1914. Bicycles were a cheap way for rapid troop movement, faster than infantry, although lacking the cross-country mobility of cavalry; they were not hampered by the need for fodder, expert care and stabling that a horse demanded.

Chapter Ten

Army Service Corps

A group of ASC non-commissioned officers on active duty wearing the standard Service Dress uniform with leather Pattern 1903 belts, PH bags and leather lace-up 'trench' boots.

Left: A nice studio portrait of an ASC private belonging to the 34th Division, distinguishable by the chequerboard insignia, a crude representation of the 'Shepherd's' tartan of the Tyneside Scottish. The four overseas stripes on the sleeve date this photograph during 1918.

An ASC signaler, probably a motorcyclist wearing a soft cap with drivers goggles. He wears the tropical issue KD frock with white over blue signalers' brassards to each arm. Note the Bedford cord drab breeches with leather reinforcements, ankle boots and leather gaiters.

Left: An ASC corporal serving with the Ammunition Column, note the cloth sign in the shape of a shell. Photographed in Poperinghe in March 1917. These men were responsible for supplying shell and ammunition to the front.

"Some of Coulston's Angels" – ASC ambulance drivers in France 1915. These men had the hazardous job of getting the wounded away from the front, often under enemy fire.

CQMS J.C. Burton. He is wearing a pre-war pattern of greatcoat with a chest pocket and cape attachment. The photograph is dated February 23rd, 1915.

An ASC Other Rank in marching order wearing a dismounted pattern greatcoat, Pattern 1903 equipment with a Pattern 1911 webbing 'other services' haversack. He wears a Pattern 1905 SD cap and a pair of rubber driver's goggles.

Above: ASC private wearing the heavy canvas 'Coat, Sheepskin lined' and equipped with SMLE, Pattern 1903 belt with ammunition pouches, water bottle and a Pattern 1911 webbing haversack as commonly issued to mounted troops.

Above right: ASC NCO's, one in a dismounted pattern greatcoat and the other in the double-breasted mounted pattern greatcoat. The photograph is dated on the reverse April 1st, 1917.

Right: ASC men wearing the heavy drivers 'Coat, Sheepskin lined' that helped keep the ASC drivers warm in their open cab Lorries. In 1918 the ASC became the RASC (Royal Army Service Corps) in recognition of their wartime work.

Left: An ASC Lorry driver wearing the 'Coat, Sheepskin lined'. The coat was made of heavy weight canvas with fur collar and lining and metal fastening clips instead of buttons. The red rubber goggles he has attached to the cap were the pattern issued to the Royal Flying Corps before the war.

Two sergeants in Russia wearing the double-breasted mounted pattern of great-coat with winter sheepskin lining. The fur hat, displaying the ASC badge, is a British made item for Arctic use. Made of seal skin fur, and Bedford cord, it is lined with heavy quilted cotton thus making it very warm. Note the special artic issue 'Shackleton' boots.

Left: Two ASC sergeants wearing the heavy padded winter coat and fur hats, that were issued to the North Russian Relief Force during the Russian Civil War. This portrait is photographed in Siberia, and dated March 1919.

"Rum". The SRD (Supply Reserve Depot) one-gallon jars were filled with a thick treacle-like liquid that was very potent. It was a frequent lifesaver for the front line troops, when it arrived! Troops consequently interpreted the initials S.R.D. as 'Seldom Reaches Destination'.

Opposite
Top: British soldiers wearing the wool lined canvas winter coats, with leather jerkins beneath for extra warmth. All are armed with the Russian 7.62 Mosin-Nagant 1891 model rifle and bayonet.

Bottom: 55th (West Lancashire) Division ASC and RAMC with a 'Bully Beef' ration dump in England, shortly before departing for France. The famous Fray Bentos bully beef, as supplied from Argentina, was the staple diet of the British Expeditionary Force. It was the ASC's responsibility to transport stores to the front.

Chapter Eleven

Royal Army Medical Corps

Private H. Cheeseman, RAMC, 48th (South Midland) Divisional in 1915. He wears standard Service Dress with a Pattern 1903 water bottle carrier and a Pattern 1908 webbing haversack.

Above: Royal Marine medical unit in service dress with neck flaps attached to their caps. All wear Pattern 1908 belts with Pattern 1903 water bottles and haversacks. The greatcoats are rolled in a horseshoe shape. The photograph is marked on the reverse "Left England, February 18th, 1916".

Right: Two RAMC men in marching order, wearing leather Pattern 1914 Infantry Equipment with brace attachments. The *Carte Postale* is dated April 9th, 1916.

Above: An RAMC man in Pattern 1914 marching order, with a box respirator and a PH gas hood bag. He wears the red on white Geneva cross which signifies a medical orderly. The device is outlined in bullion on a black background.

Right: An RAMC corporal, photographed in Poperinghe, wearing a Pattern 1914 belt with unfastened brace attachments. These were introduced in December 1915 to enable the Pattern 1914 Infantry Equipment to be worn by unarmed Units.

Opposite
Left: A medical orderly from the Royal Engineers. He carries a medical orderly's satchel that contained the basic medical equipment required in the field.

Right: An orderly in Pattern 1903 marching order with rolled greatcoat carried in bandolier fashion. Note the Victorian Pattern 1882 belt. The only concession yet made to the tropical climate is the Wolseley Pattern helmet.

Above: RAMC orderly's wearing the simplified pattern of khaki drill frock with stand collar and pointed pocket flaps. They wear Pattern 1914 equipment in marching order with the large pack.

Above right: A photograph that shows the KD frock, Wolseley and medics brassard being worn. The brassard, or armband is stamped 'ARMY MEDICAL SERVICE' and has the standard Geneva Red Cross device. The KD frock is a wartime simplified jacket, first issued in late 1915.

Right: RAMC personnel wearing Wolseley helmets with their cap badges attached to the puggaree. This card had been posted from Alexandria, Egypt on June 2nd, 1915. On the back is written, "You will notice the sun helmet is the only installment we have so far towards a tropical uniform".

Left: A Territorial RAMC private with steel helmet and PH bag. He wears the Red Cross brassard on his left arm and the circular red on white Geneva cross that signifies a medical orderly on the arm. He holds the early War Office Pattern 'Brodie' steel helmet with raw edge. The photograph is dated January 24th, 1917.

Above: A RAMC corporal wearing a 1916 (Mark I) 'Brodie' steel helmet with cover. The pattern is distinguishable by a single piece chinstrap and rimmed edge, first issued during the latter half of 1916. Just visible is a shell dressing safety pin attached to his helmet. Dated on the reverse October 3rd, 1916.

Left: RAMC London Territorial lance-corporals in France. Note that the tall man with the steel helmet is wearing a pair of khaki drill shorts, a practice brought back from India. This photograph was probably taken during summer of 1916.

Left: A RAMC sergeant in Pattern 1914 Infantry Equipment with steel helmet, box respirator and PH bag. Note the makeshift photo studio with simple sheet backdrop, commonly seen in many *Carte Postale* photographs taken on the Western Front.

Opposite
Left: RAMC Regimental Sergeant Major (RSM), note the Royal Crest badge on the arm that denotes the rank of RSM or Warrant Officer I Class. He wears a standard 1902 SD Jacket, an issue two-piece helmet cover and box respirator. RSM's were permitted to wear the Sam Browne and often wore officer quality jackets.

Right: A Territorial RAMC Captain in cuff rank jacket, sandbag covered helmet and a PH bag. To help deflect any shine whilst in the trenches, helmets were purposely covered in anything from mud to woolen, khaki drill and hessian sandbag covers. They were commercially available for officers and later became part of the issued kit, however many were just field-made from British or French sandbags.

3739

Above: RAMC Field Ambulance officers, photographed in Arras c.1917. They are all in Sam Browne order and carry small box respirator satchels. One officer wears a 'British Warm' coat.

Below: RAMC men from the 48th (South Midland) Division, in France. They wear winter fur coats and carry the box respirators in the alert position. All ranks within two miles of the frontline where ordered to carry their respirators in the alert position, fastened to the chest with opened flap.

A RAMC section by a 10-ton train carriage in France. They are all wearing Pattern 1914 Infantry Equipment with brace attachments instead of ammo pouches, steel helmets and carry two PH gas hoods each. The specialist brace attachments were introduced in late December 1915 to enable the Pattern 1914 equipment to be worn by unarmed units.

Wrapped up warm for the winter – RAMC men in France, marked "Xmas 1914".

An RAMC Field Ambulance photographed in 1917. The first point of call was the Regimental Aid Post before casualties were taken to the Field Ambulance and Advanced Dressing Stations. Wounded could then be evacuated via Casualty Clearing Stations to Field Hospitals.

A relaxed group of men with beer and cigarettes. Note the man wearing the shorts, most probably cut down from a pair of drab serge SD trousers. This practice was popular during the summer months on the Western Front, but were soon discouraged and finally prohibited by a General Routine Order in October 1916.

Chapter Twelve

Royal Engineers

Corporals from a Royal Engineers Signal Section. They wear Pattern 1903 pistol kit, in light marching order with rolled greatcoats in bandolier fashion and SD caps with driver's goggles.

"Off to the Front, 1914" Royal Engineer signalers in marching order wearing Pattern 1903 bandoliers, water bottles with rolled greatcoats and groundsheets. Note the white over blue signalers brassards.

An RE Signal Service group with telephony and signals equipment, 1915. The telephone sets are the portable type 'D' Mk.III models. The Signal Service was formed in 1912 to take over responsibility for all communications within a force up to and including infantry battalion and cavalry regiment headquarters.

Left: Signaler F. Colman. This photograph clearly shows the stitched peak of the soft cap as issued in 1916. The stitching on the peak and cap band was done to add more rigidity to the cap. Note the cloth 'RE' title, signaler's brassard and four overseas stripes, c.1918.

An engineer in Pattern 1908 equipment in marching order, with box respirator and SMLE. Note the method of carrying the infantry pattern 'D' shape mess-tin on the haversack.

Left: An engineer wearing an early pattern of KD frock, distinguishable by the stand and fall collar and pointed pockets. He is issued with the Wolseley Pattern tropical helmet with its muslin puggaree. The puggaree served little function apart from decorative dress.

Left: Five sappers on the Somme, c.1916. Note the engineer at the back is wearing an Australian Pattern 1908/15 leather belt.

Above: A summer Western Front photograph of RE sergeants, two wearing MM ribbons. The man sitting is wearing serge SD shorts. In mid-1917 a pattern of shorts, or knickers as they were officially called was approved for service dress wear. Note the Pattern 1908 shoulder brace being worn as a walking-out belt.

Left: 'The Mounted Bricklayers', a popular Royal Engineer nickname. A mounted engineer in winter goatskin coat, Pattern 1903 bandolier and a PH gas helmet bag worn over the shoulder, winter 1916.

Opposite
Left: "Dad, France 1915" Signaler Bishop wearing a winter issue 'teddy bear' fur coat, Pattern 1903 bandolier, SD cap and is armed with the universal issue SMLE No.1 Mk.III 303-inch rifle.

Right: A Royal Engineers officer in a cuff rank jacket with leather 'trench' boots and a fawn colored winter service trench cap. This pattern of cap became hugely popular with officers in 1915 and 1916.

Two Royal Engineer Tunnelling officers. Note the man on the left is wearing an other ranks jacket, nicknamed by officers a 'Tommy' jacket, after the popular 'Tommy Atkins' slang name for the British soldier.

Royal Engineer Tunnelling officers at 'Proto' School. Tunnelling officers and men were trained in the use of mine rescue apparatus and protection against gas in mining, as shown here with 'PROTO' breathing apparatus.

Part of a Royal Engineers Field Company photographed at Fringes in France, 1918. They all wear Pattern 1908 equipment and armed with SMLE's. The officer wears a cuff rank jacket with Sam Browne belt.

Two signalers pose with a Fray Bentos bully beef tin and wine. The name Fray Bentos was the trademark of a large Argentinean beef company, the major supplier to the British Expeditionary Force.

Opposite
Top: A group of engineers in shirt-sleeve order, wearing grey-back flannel shirts, Gor'blimey caps and Pattern 1903 bandoliers. Note the man on extreme left has the pre-war Pattern 1906 aluminum dog tag attached to his braces. The postcard, passed by censor No.689, was sent by Field Post Office in October 1915.

Bottom: A group of Royal Engineer signalers wearing light tan leather jerkins, tin hats, Pattern 1903 bandoliers and signaler white over blue brassards. The photograph is dated 1917.

Chapter Thirteen

Royal Flying Corps

A studio portrait of a Royal Flying Corps (RFC) pilot officer wearing the officers Pattern 1912 'Maternity' jacket. He wears cloth pips to denote rank of captain, a pilot's wing brevet and a medal ribbon.

A captured flying officer photographed at the Trier POW camp in 1918. He wears a Pattern 1912 SD Jacket. This style of jacket was officially introduced in November 1913 (Army Order 378), and nicknamed the 'Maternity', as it was said to resemble clothing worn by expectant mothers.

Pilot William Percy Parker, 2nd Squadron, RFC. He went to France on August 12th, 1914, and received the French *Medaille Militaire* award for gallantry two weeks later. He wears the early issue Pattern 1912 'Maternity' jacket without shoulder straps. The standard 'ROYAL FLYING CORPS' cloth titles are worn with early pattern gilt-metal pilots wings.

A young second-lieutenant posted to the Royal Flying Corps from the East Kent Regiment (Buffs). He wears an officer's cuff rank jacket with cloth RFC pilot wings and bronzed collar dogs denoting the Buffs. He also wears the Field Service forage cap as adopted by the RFC in 1913. Officers continued to wear the uniform of their original regiment until officially gazetted.

An RFC pilot in a maternity jacket showing cloth RFC wings and medal ribbons. He wears the forage cap that became as much an *esprit de corps* item of clothing for the RFC as the maternity jacket.

Lieutenant Harry Wise, RFC, was killed on January 13th, 1918. He wears an RFC forage cap, a single-breasted army/RND style jacket with naval cuff lace, shoulder rank pips and cloth RFC wings. The admiralty officially recognized this jacket in November 1916, although it had been widely worn by the RNAS prior to that.

A studio portrait of Flight Sub-Lieutenant Kenneth Hooper, 'B' Squadron, 2nd Wing RNAS in 1916. He is wearing the distinctive naval dark blue double-breasted jacket, nicknamed the 'Monkey Jacket', with gold rank lace on the cuffs with a gold eagle to denote a pilot. He also wears the dark blue naval cap with RNAS badge.

Opposite
Top left: An Australian Flying Corps (AFC) lieutenant wearing an army shoulder rank uniform, with bronzed rising sun collar dogs, bronzed pips, and embroidered 'AUSTRALIA' shoulder titles and 'AFC' wings.

Bottom left: Second-Lieutenant Frederick Philip Pemble, 213th Squadron, RAF, photographed in the khaki RAF jacket with cloth belt. Written on the back it says "going to 213th Squadron Dunkirk tomorrow morning: will write soon, love Phil". Pemble was killed whilst flying on June 29th, 1918. The photograph is dated May 25th, 1918

Right: An AFC second-lieutenant wearing the shoulder rank uniform with trench cap. On the reverse is written "May Madge you darling V.A.D., have many happy days and spend a few with me. My thoughts will oft times stray back, even when over the Hun lines – Happy memories ever yours, Charles 1918".

COPYRIGHT

Above: A RAF captain showing details of the cap. The cap is similar in style to the RNAS pattern of cap with khaki crown and a black glazed peak and chinstrap and a black mohair band to which is fixed the RAF badge and gilt rank bars. The RAF badge is entwined with laurel leaves, a crown and a metal bird, similar to that worn by the RNAS on the sleeve. The rank bars, one for lieutenant and two for captain, were eradicated in July 1918. Field and General officers wore rows of gold oak leaves on the peak to denote rank.

Right: A sergeant pilot wearing the drab serge Pattern 1912 'Maternity' jacket with 'ROYAL FLYING CORPS' titles, sergeant chevrons with the four bladed propeller. The maternity jacket was officially labeled 'Jackets, SD, RFC'.

Opposite
"Lt. Maude, met in C.C.S, July 1918". Note the characteristics of the Royal Air Force (RAF) pattern uniform without shoulder straps, four gilt RAF buttons, two breast patch pockets, two large bellow hip pockets and a buckled fabric waist belt in lieu of the Sam Browne. Rank was worn not only on the cuffs like the Royal Navy, but also on the peaked cap in the form of gilt bars.

A super photograph of an 'Old Contemptible' pilot, Sergeant E.J. Street, 4th Squadron, RFC. He drove down a German Taube on August 26th, 1914, and landed to attempt its capture, but the enemy burnt the machine. He was awarded the *Medaille Militaire* for work during August 1914, being commissioned later in July 1916.

A second-lieutenant observer in a RFC maternity. Shoulder straps were introduced on the maternity jacket in June 1914 with some other minor modifications. He too wears the standard forage cap, introduced into the RFC in 1913. This was also sometimes referred too as the 'Austrian' pattern. The folding side-cap had a band, which could be let down to form a type of balaclava helmet fastening with two small buttons under the chin.

A second-lieutenant observer attached to the Royal Flying Corps from the Durham Light Infantry. He retains the DLI collar dogs on his army pattern cuff rank jacket, but also wears a RFC badged forage hat. Notice the 'O' for observer wing brevet on his left breast.

Right: A sergeant observer wearing a drab serge maternity jacket with an observer cloth brevet.

A sergeant observer wearing the 1902 SD jacket with an observer wing brevet. Manufacture of the maternity jacket ended to coincide with the creation of the Royal Air Force in April 1918.

A 1918 dated photograph of a sergeant observer. He wears the Pattern 1902 SD with a soft cap. This style of army jacket replaced the maternity when RFC clothing stocks came to an end.

An RAF observer wearing the drab serge RAF pattern jacket with buttoned cloth belt. It was officially called 'Jacket, Khaki, Pattern 1918, Version 2', and remained working dress until about 1923. He also wears the khaki RAF cap with black band to which is attached an embroidered RAF badge of an eagle in flight. At the top of the sleeves are red on khaki embroidered RAF eagles with out-stretched neck and wings. The 'DR' cloth badge is that of a Dispatch Rider.

RFC airmen wearing the standard SD cap with the early Pattern 1912 'Maternity' jacket with no shoulder straps, vertical slit pockets and pointed cuff-tightening tabs. This style jacket was abolished in June 1914 when the pockets were changed to a horizontal type, the shoulder straps added whilst the cuff tabs were eradicated. Both wear the Pattern 1903 'pistol' equipment and are armed with 4-inch barreled Webley Mk.IV service revolvers.

"Somewhere in France".

An RFC airman in a maternity with the abbreviated pattern of 'R.F.C.' cloth title that originated in August 1915. The photograph was taken in France, and dated May 6th, 1916.

"Somewhere in France 1916".

Right: Two airmen wearing the Pattern 1908 equipment with brace attachments. These were worn to support the weight on the revolver and ammunition pouch. Note the pistol lanyards.

Airmen from 24th Squadron, pose against a simple blanket backdrop in France. They wear the standard Pattern 1908 belt, with leather ammunition pouches and holsters that contain the general service issue .455-inch Webley revolver.

Above: A fine portrait of an RFC airman wearing the Royal Stewart tartan 'battle patch' for the 15th (Scottish) Division, c.1916. RFC personnel were seconded to divisional headquarters for purposes of providing a communication link between ground and air services, e.g. spotting for the artillery.

Right: An RFC airman wearing the universal Pattern 1902 SD jacket with 'ROYAL FLYING CORPS' cloth insignia. The Service Dress cap is the standard soft pattern with a brass RFC badge.

Opposite: A South Lancashire Regiment sergeant with two RFC First Class Air Mechanics, distinguishable by the two-bladed propeller, as introduced in October 1916. The flyer on the right wears an observer wing, unusually sewn onto the centre of his jacket instead of the left breast. All three carry the box respirator satchel.

Above: A sergeant wearing the RAF serge Pattern 1918 jacket with buttoned cloth belt. Notice the medal ribbons and wound stripe.

Above right: Two airmen in maternity jackets and slouch hats. Slouch hats were not just common to the Australians, but worn widely by the British, especially in Salonika and Palestine.

Right: Flight-Sergeant Frank Morgan of the Australian Flying Corps (AFC). He wears the Australian SD Jacket without cloth belt and metal 'AFC' and 'AUSTRALIA' shoulder titles. Sewn to his jacket are sergeant chevrons, a four-bladed propeller and an AFC cloth patch.

A mix of RFC, RAMC and ASC men photographed in France, May 11th, 1915. The ASC drivers are issued with the early RFC pattern goggles that were made out of a red rubber frame with an elastic strap. Initially for flying, they were relegated by the autumn of 1915 for use by dispatch riders and transport drivers. Some were even used as an early form of protection against gas attack.

Standing by a Sopwith Tri-plane named "Hilda" are a group of RNAS men wearing a variety of service dress including the Pattern 1902 and 'simplified' jackets. The two Chief Petty Officers are wearing officer quality service dress. The photograph dates from 1917.

Left: An RFC airman wearing a rubberized double breasted driver's coat. This pattern of coat was issued to men in exposed positions who were open to the elements. Note the goggles on his forage hat. This photograph is dated April 11th, 1917.

The RFC corporal is wearing the Pattern 1913 other ranks maternity greatcoat. This was made of thick serge cloth, and cut in the maternity style with its fly-fastening lapel. The greatcoat was modified, as with the jacket, in June 1914 to add shoulder straps. Notice the black enamel fronted aviators' wristwatch.

A First Class Air-Mechanic. He wears the Pattern 1913 'Maternity' greatcoat with Pattern 1908 'pistol' equipment in marching order with brace attachments. Just visible at the rear is a circular cavalry pattern mess-tin that was widely used by the RFC.

This RFC airman wears the Pattern 1913 greatcoat, steel helmet and Pattern 1908 'pistol' equipment. He wears dispatch riders leather 'trench' boots and mounted pattern 'pantaloon' breeches.

Above: A studio portrait of Second-Lieutenant Herbert Hardy, dated August 25th, 1917. He wears the maternity jacket, with bronzed RFC collar dogs. Over this he wears a 'Trench Coat' as supplied by outfitters like Burberrys and Robinson & Cleaver.

Above right: RNAS Sub-Lieutenant C.H. Butterworth, 3rd Wing RNAS. Butterworth was shot down and taken prisoner when his Sopwith Strutter was forced to land whilst on a raid to a German Mauser Factory.

Right: Lieutenant Percy Reginald Cann, 65th Squadron RFC. He wears a RFC forage cap and a winter fleece lined 'British Warm' woolen coat. Cann was shot down whilst flying a Sopwith Camel, and died of wounds on April 2nd, 1918.

A group of RFC officers in France wearing a wide range of coats, including the Burberrys 'Trench Coat' and 'Tielocken' with a selection of 'British Warms'. Major Lanoe Hawker VC, DSO, Commanding 24th Squadron is standing in the back row, second from left. Hawker was shot down and killed on November 23rd, 1916, after a 35-minute duel with the infamous Manfred von Richthofen, the 'Red Baron'.

Left: Second Class Air-Mechanic F.G. Rumsey Williams, August 1914. He wears the early Pattern 1913 short flying coat and also the early issue high domed 'Warren' helmet, which was sealed as a pattern in August 1914. The Warren was not popular and soon relegated for training purposes.

Sergeant Bennett, marked on the reverse "No.1 RFC Reserve 1914". Bennett was wounded in the leg whilst flying a contact patrol with 15th Squadron in May 1917. He holds the French manufactured 'Roold' pattern helmet that was accepted for issue and sealed as a pattern in May 1914, and used extensively by the RFC during the first year of the war.

Sergeant Arthur Sanderson in 1916 wearing the Pattern 1913 short leather flying coat with flying helmet and goggles. This fleece lined thigh length coat had a crossover chest piece, two flapped pockets on the skirt and a small angled map chest pocket. A matching pair of leather trousers was also made available with this coat that had a distinctive front flap opening.

Right: A flyer wearing the long pattern aviator's coat with leather flying gauntlets, a 'Cowl' type flying helmet and 'Triplex' safely goggles. There was a huge array of flying clothing available for purchase that was sold through private outfitters like Dunhills, Gamages, Harrods and Robinson & Cleaver.

The 'Cowl' type helmet is clearly shown in this photograph, commonly worn by the observer as opposed to the pilot. He wears the long pattern leather flying coat with plain leather gauntlets.

Above: A nice studio portrait of an observer in full flying kit. He wears the long pattern flying coat with slanted map pocket clearly visible. This rare image shows an early wireless voice-radio headset fitted into his flying helmet, the jack for which he holds in his bearskin gloves.

Above right: Lieutenant Samuel Cook, Middlesex Regiment, attached Royal Air Force in 1918. He wears a long pattern flyers coat, bearskin gloves and holds a standard leather flying helmet.

Right: A pilot standing on the snowy ground wearing a 'Sidcot' flying suit, 'Cowl' helmet, flip-back mitten gauntlets and a pair of 'Fug' boots. The thigh-length sheepskin boots were invented by Major Lanoe Hawker VC, DSO and sealed as 'Boots, Thigh' in December 1916.

A flyer from 'A' Flight, 27th Squadron, RFC with his Martinsyde G100 aircraft. He wears a short pattern flying coat and 'Fug' boots. Note the elephant shield on the fuselage, the squadron emblem, and the aerial camera and armament of Lewis machine-guns.

Above: Lieutenant Esplin (pilot) and Lieutenant Needham (observer) in what appears to be a DH9A. With poor pilot training and experience, and with aircraft often suffering from poor mechanics and structural design, many crashed even without contact with the enemy.

Below: A dawn patrol after its return showing a variety of flying gear, including 'Sidcots' and long pattern flying coats. Note the gauntlet gloves with attached fleece-lined mittens stitched to the back of the hand that could be held back by a press-stud when dexterity was required. These were popular with many flyers.

A fine photograph of a flight sub-lieutenant in a RNAS pattern coat with 'Fug' boots. Many RNAS officers adopted black flying coats and helmets instead of brown, the coats being more often than not cut in the double-breasted style like their uniforms.

Flight Sub-Lieutenant R.G. Gardner in 1918, wearing a RNAS pattern leather flight coat, flying cap and goggles. RNAS flying clothing was commonly made in black leather.

Opposite
Left: This flyer is wearing the dark blue naval double-breasted woolen greatcoat with black leather flying helmet and early rubberized goggles. This coat was introduced in May 1915 to be worn as flying kit. It is distinguishable by the huge flap hip pockets. Note the red on blue 'R.N.A.S' cloth to the top of the sleeve and also the Leading Rating naval arm badge. The photograph is dated June 1915.

Right: An observer with pistol kit, scarf and 'Cowl' flying helmet with goggles. It was common in the early flying years for pilots and observers to fly with sidearms, rifles and even shotguns before aircraft were armed with Lewis or Vickers machine-guns.

Above: An RFC corporal in an army mounted Pattern 1902 double-breasted greatcoat, with a flying helmet crowned by an RFC cap badge and 'Triplex' safety-glass goggles.

Above right: An early image of a corporal in the maternity style greatcoat with flying helmet, and first pattern rubber flying goggles. He also wears fur-backed flying gauntlets to help protect the hands from the extreme cold temperatures experienced at altitudes in open cockpits.

Right: The 'Sidcot' was invented by Flight Sub-Lieutenant Sidney Cotton, 3rd Wing RNAS. It was made of an outer layer of proofed khaki twill over a rubberized muslin inner lining and a mohair liner. It also had a chest map pocket and two knee pockets. The pattern was soon adopted by the RFC and sealed in December 1917. The Sidcot soon replaced leather flying gear and became the classic late war flying suit.

Opposite
Top left: A corporal in the maternity style greatcoat with flying helmet, fingered leather gauntlet gloves, and flying goggles. The cap style flying helmets were popular with pilots and not too dissimilar in design to the standard motoring caps of the time.

Top right: A sergeant observer photographed in a studio in Cairo, Egypt. He is wearing a fur-lined leather flying helmet and 'Triplex' goggles.

Below: Flying officers at Biggin Hill, England 1918. Photographed towards the end of the war this image shows the variety of officer's uniform still in use at the time.

'C Flight', 16th Squadron, RAF in July 1918. This group photograph shows a wide range of uniform from the Pattern 1912 'Maternity' jackets, the standard army cuff and shoulder rank jackets through to the newer style RAF uniform.

53rd Squadron, RAF in France, November 1918. On April 1st, 1918 the RFC and RNAS were combined to form the world's largest and first independent air service, called the Royal Air Force. Even with the forming of the RAF in April 1918 officers were still permitted to wear their old uniforms as working dress within the confines of their own aerodromes. It was not until after the First World War and demobilization that the blue RAF service dress was universally worn.

Chapter Fourteen

Miscellaneous

"Vive l'Angleterre! Vive la France!" – RAMC men hat swapping with French troops from the 12th (Territorial) Infantry Regiment. Photographed by a café in Amiens, 1914.

Marked on the back, "Souvenir of a short stay at Abbeville, whilst on active service, Oct 1914". Abbeville was a detraining point before the London Scottish, photographed here, moved into action during the First Battle of Ypres. Highland dress proved somewhat of an amusement for the French. The London Scottish wore a plain hodden grey kilt and a blue tourie, badge backing and hose-top flashes.

Entente Cordiale at the Café De La Caserne in Peronne, 1917 – British Tommy's from the 56th (London) Division with French *Poilus* from the *17ième Régiment d'Infanterie* and the *Chasseurs Alpins*, outside the establishment owned by the Marcolle family.

Salute! Men from the Army Service Corps having drinks with staff from Café Buvette, owned by L. Goudard, 1916. An *Estaminet* like this one, were cafés that offered cheap brandy or wine and *omelette et frites* to the troops when out of the line.

"Café 'Do Drop' in, English Spoken, Lancashire Understood". An Expeditionary Force Canteen (EFC) in France. The EFC started life in 1894 when three officers, dissatisfied with the food supply for soldiers, formed the Canteen & Mess Co-operative Society (CMCS). In 1915 the CMCS helped form the EFC, later in 1917 to become the Army Canteen Committee. In 1918 the RN joined and the name changed to the Navy & Army Canteen Board. At the end of the war the RAF joined. In January 1921, after a review by Churchill the name was changed to the Navy, Army and Air Force Institute, the NAAFI.

Left: Helpers from the British Army's Expeditionary Force Canteen. The personnel belonged to the ASC, and wore the same service dress as the rest of the British Army. This photograph shows two different variations of the 'EFC' metal title.

"Salonika 1918" A Regimental Military Police lance corporal from the 10th Battalion, Hampshire Regiment. He wears a soft cap, service dress jacket, red on black 'MP' brassard and the Pattern 1903 pistol holster on a shoulder strap for extra support. This was a popular way of supporting the weight of the pistol in the military police.

Left: A Military Police (MP) lance corporal, wearing a 'MP' brassard with issue Pattern 1903 'pistol' equipment, a whistle chain and simplified SD jacket. The red cap cover, which gave the Military Police the nickname 'Redcaps' began to be issued in 1916, but was not generally worn unless high visibility was necessary. In an attack the Redcaps were used to set up 'stragglers' posts' immediately behind the frontline to collect and sort deserters or others leaving the line unauthorized. Over 300 British soldiers were executed during the First World War for deserting or similar offences.

Left: A Military Policeman. He wears a soft cap with Service Dress jacket, 'MP' brassard and a Pattern 1903 webbing belt as introduced in the spring of 1917. The MP's and Provost's responsibilities were to arrest any soldier found without a pass, plundering, making unlawful requisitions, or committing any other offences of any kind.

A winter photograph of a Regimental Policemen or Provost with a 'RMP' brassard, protected from the cold and wet by a leather jerkin and a covered Gor'blimey. The photo is dated January 21st, 1916. Provosts, not to be confused with MPs, were mainly detailed to carry out police work within their own battalion.

Left: Military Police corporals in 1918. Note the Military Mounted Police 'MMP' shoulder titles, sewn on 'MMP' titles and 'MP' cloth brassards. Note the equipment in pistol order with single cross strap.

Above: Regimental Military Police (RMP) from the 2/6th Battalion, East Surrey Regiment. All provosts in this photograph wear the 'RMP' brassard on their lower right arm of what is their standard service dress uniform. In 1917 'RMP' was changed to 'RP' for Regimental Police.

Left: Men from the Army Veterinary Corps (AVC) in France. They are wearing Pattern 1903 Bandolier Equipment, except the sergeant who is in pistol order. Note the Gor'blimey cap cover and trench boots. This photograph would date from early 1915.

Opposite
Communication on the wing. Signalers from the 145th Brigade, 48th (South Midland) Division with their carrier pigeons. Where field telephones, runners, dispatch riders and visual signaling by flag, lamp or mirror failed, pigeons were a solution. By 1918 there were 20,000 birds with personnel of some 380 experts. The 'Pigeoneers' went over the top with their birds carried in 'Assault Baskets', ready to send important messages back to HQ.

Left: A goat mascot of the 4th Mobile Veterinary Section, AVC, who was born on April 22nd, 1915 under shellfire. This was the opening date of the Second Battle of Ypres when the Germans first used poison gas in warfare.

A British Red Cross worker in France wearing a drab serge uniform and an enameled Geneva Red Cross badge on his soft cap. The uniform is styled on the British service dress.

Left: A Non Combatant Corps (NCC) soldier. After the passing of the Military Service Act in early 1916 the NCC was formed, comprising of conscientious objectors. They were used for work on roads, hutments, timber work, quarrying, sanitary duties, and handling supplies. Eight companies existed by the middle of June 1916.

14th (London Scottish) Battalion, London Regimental Band with pipes and drums in Arras, 1918. In battle the traditional role of bandsmen was to help the RAMC and act as stretcher-bearers for the battalion.

A Territorial RAMC band in France, c.1916. Note the musicians' pouches, including cases for flutes and also the bags that would contain the brass instruments. Most regiments and corps had their own band, and took their instruments with them on active service.

Above: Regimental Band of the 6th Battalion, Seaforth Highlanders on the Somme, autumn 1915.

Left: A mounted South Nottingham Hussars trooper. The horse is equipped with regulation Pattern 1912 saddle with a Pattern 1899 sword carried on the nearside of his saddle. His greatcoat and personal items are rolled in a groundsheet and strapped to the front arch of the saddle with his circular cavalry pattern mess-tin. His ammunition is carried in the leather Pattern 1903 bandolier and belt pouches.

Opposite
Top: Regulation saddlery consisting of a Pattern 1908 sword; fastened to the sword scabbard are a canvas bucket for watering and a post for picketing the horse; he carries a rolled groundsheet strapped to the front arch of the saddle, and a rolled greatcoat to the rear arch. His ammunition is carried in the leather Pattern 1903 bandolier and belt pouches, and he carries a water bottle, binoculars and webbing haversack. A cavalryman was more a mounted infantryman and carried everything necessary for him to fight as an infantryman once his horse has been led to the rear.

Bottom left: A trooper from the 12th (Prince of Wales's Royal) Lancers with his mount. Note the issue fly veil and Pattern 1894 lance with ash stave. He is also armed with the SMLE carried in its leather 'Bucket, Rifle' and a 90-round Pattern 1903 bandolier. Both cavalry and yeomanry were commonly issued with the 90-round bandolier instead of the 50-round version.

Bottom right: Trooper C.J. Carroll, Royal Canadian Dragoons in France, November 1916. On the reverse is written, "please don't laugh at the poor photo". He is armed with the regulation straight bladed Pattern 1908 sword and carries the Pattern 1903 90-round bandolier. A second bandolier was often issued, and worn around the horse's neck.

A profile photograph showing the Pattern 1912 Universal Steel Arch Saddle with Pattern 1902 bridle. Attached to the saddle is a canvas watering bucket, nosebag and cavalry pattern mess-tin. A rolled blanket is strapped to the rear arch, whilst a greatcoat and groundsheet are strapped to the front arch of the saddle above the pair of leather wallets. The Pattern 1908 sword is fastened to a leather scabbard horseshoe case. Note also the leather wire-cutter pouch.

16th (The Queen's) Lancers in France, c.1918. The lance was still classified as a weapon of war in 1918 and not officially relegated to ceremonial use until 1927. In this modern war the value of both lance and sword declined quickly in favor of the rifle and machine-gun.

Above: A cavalry warrant officer dressed in a winter goat or sheepskin waistcoat, rubber 'gum' boots, gloves and an issued four-piece sacking cover on his steel helmet. The crossed swords metal badge on the sleeve denotes the best swordsman skill-at-arms award.

Above right: A wounded Cheshire captain using what looks like overseas stripes on his left sleeve. He has a 1914-15 campaign ribbon on his chest. The 1914 and 1914-15 Stars were sanctioned in 1917 for overseas service during these years. He wears a light blue armband to denote his status as a hospital patient. Officers where permitted to wear their service dress whilst convalescing.

Right: Wounded New Zealanders from the 14th (South Otago Rifles) Regiment in 'Hospital blues'. The uniform, light blue, white shirt with a red tie was worn by all those convalescing from wounds back in dear old 'Blighty' (the nickname given to Britain by the troops, from the Hindustani '*belati*', meaning a distant country). The uniform was commonly worn by patients exercising on the hospital grounds or on a day pass from the hospital.

Right: Corporal G.H. Whitlock, 1st (Cape Province) Battalion, South African Infantry, at Lewisham Military Hospital, October 14th, 1916. He was wounded July 18th, 1916 at Delville Wood on the Somme. Although wearing of the blues uniform was compulsory, the soldier could still retain his service headgear for wear.

Opposite
Top left: Back from the battlefields, wounded soldiers pose with a nurse. All are wearing the 'Hospital blues' uniform with their standard headdress. Note the man on the right is wearing hospital issue slippers.

Top right: South African wounded convalescing in England. Note the 'South Africa' shoulder title on the greatcoats and light blue brassard on the right arm that denotes the soldier as a hospital patient. The blues uniform is just visible underneath the coats.

Bottom left: Wounded Australian troops convalescing in Britain in 1916. They are wearing two different variations of the 'Hospital blues' uniform, designed not only to mark out the man as having 'done his bit', but also giving him a comfortable and practical outfit that was easily distinguishable by medical staff.

Botom right: "Some of Britons sons of metal that the enemy's fire could not melt". Wounded soldiers in greatcoats that show the light blue 'convalescing' brassard being worn. The three different patterns of wartime greatcoats are shown here.

Right: Two wounded West Yorkshire soldiers pose with cigarettes, one from the West Yorkshire Regiment, the other from the West Riding Regiment. Just visible under the greatcoat is the 'Hospital blues' uniform. With this uniform the standard regimental headdress and cap badge was worn, as seen in this photograph.

Above: Sister Gedge of the Queen Alexandra's Imperial Military Nursing Service (Reserve), c.1916. The nursing sister wears the traditional grey and red service dress uniform with cape ('tippet') and cap ('veil') of the QAIMNS.

Right: Ella Heptinstall, photographed in January 1918. She wears a leather buttoned woolen coat with cloth crossover belt, lace-up boots and a brimmed hat with badge of the Women's Army Auxiliary Corps (WAAC). Note the signalers brassard that denotes a telegraphist's role in a signals office. The WAAC's were also employed to tend war graves, cook, bake bread and waitress.

Above: A woman wearing the uniform of the Women's Royal Air Force (WRAF). They came into being on April 1, 1918 when the RAF was created. By the Armistice about 30,000 were in the service, until disbanded on April 1st, 1920. The white 'I' patch denotes the 'Immobiles', who were personnel recruited and employed locally near the aerodromes.

Right: Worker M. Steele in August 1917 in the uniform of Queen Mary's Army Auxiliary Corps, better known as the WAAC's. They were formed in March 1917 to undertake essential behind the lines work with the Army abroad and at home, thereby releasing able-bodied men for active service. By April 1918 the Corps became the Queen Mary's Army Auxiliary Corps in recognition of their valuable work.

Above: A captured soldier from the Queen's Own Cameron Highlanders in a Prisoner of War (POW) pattern uniform. The uniform, based on the service dress, was a dark blue/black in color and had a light brown piece of cloth sewn into the left arm, down the trouser seam and also around the cap band. Most uniforms were supplied by Britain, whilst others were made by Germany, often out of ersatz material.

Above right: A group of British POWs in German captivity. This photograph shows details of the brown armband and trouser stripe. This was designed to render the prisoner more conspicuous in the event of an escape.

Right: A Cameronian sergeant wearing an army Long Service and Good Conduct medal. The ribbon is crimson with a white stripe on each end. Prior to 1917 it was plain crimson, which was found too similar to the ribbon of the Victoria Cross, thus changed.

Above: A British signaler wearing the French *Medaille Militaire* award. Many British troops were awarded foreign decorations for distinguished service and gallantry; these also included the *Croix de Guerre* and *Legion de Honour*. The ribbons of these medals were permitted to be worn on the service dress by General Routine Order 254.

Above right: A Rifle Brigade sergeant wearing a Military Medal (MM). He wears the Pattern 1902 SD jacket and Pattern 1905 SD cap, with black buttons and a black chinstrap to denote a rifle regiment. The MM was instituted in March 1916 as an award for NCOs and men of the army for acts of bravery under fire.

Right: A soldier from the 1st Battalion, Dorset Regiment wearing a Distinguished Conduct Medal (DCM) and Military Medal (MM) with Bar. The bar signifies a second award of this medal. The DCM was instituted in 1854 during the Crimean War to recognize distinguished, gallant and good conduct.

A KOSB sergeant from the 29th Division wearing a DCM and Belgian *Croix de Guerre*. The French also had a version of the *Croix de Guerre*. Note the red, half diamond divisional sign whose origin was intended as a reminder to the Division of the advantage of the diamond formation in open fighting. As the badge was worn on each shoulder, the wearer actually wore one diamond.

Sergeant Harry Wood, 2nd Battalion, Scots Guards wearing a VC, MM and 1914 'Mons' Star. He won his Victoria Cross on October 13th, 1918 in France. When an advance was desperately opposed and the streets of the village were raked by fire, Corporal Wood's platoon sergeant was killed and he took command of the leading platoon. The River Selle had to be crossed and the ruined bridge gained, although the space in front of it was full of snipers, so the corporal carried a very large brick into the open space, lay down behind it and, firing continuously on the snipers, covered his men while they worked their way across. Later in the day he repeatedly drove off enemy counter-attacks. The VC, instituted in 1856, is the highest British award for acts of outstanding gallantry.

Chapter Fifteen

Battle Insignia

A Royal Fusiliers private with slip-on white-on-khaki 'RF' cloth titles. Issued early on in the war, this pattern of cloth title was issued for the shoulder straps to wear in place of metal titles, although many units chose to sew them directly onto the jacket.

"People here are thinking of clearing out since the mayor told them the Germans might bombard the town. Will write you in a day or so. Billy". A Territorial NCO scout from the Sherwood Yeomanry. Note the *Fleur-de-Lys* First Class Scout badge, three five-pointed TF Proficiency stars and marksman cross-rifles on the lower sleeve.

Above: 8th Battalion, Kings Shropshire Light Infantry bomber with a Military Medal ribbon. The black colored shoulder stripe denotes the 22nd Division. The bomber's skill-at-arms badge on the right arm is khaki drab with a red flame, as introduced in 1915.

Above right: A Somerset Light Infantry Other Rank from the 8th Battalion, 37th Division. This Division wore a gold horseshoe on the upper arm, and colored unit patches to denote the brigade, battalion and company.

Right: Sergeant P. Durston, 13th Battalion, Rifle Brigade, with cloth horseshoe, triangle and shoulder band insignia. As a member of a rifle regiment he wears black insignia and buttons on his service dress. The horseshoe sign is that of the 37th Division.

CSM Fred Hands, 2/6th Battalion, North Staffordshire Regiment, 176th Infantry Brigade, 59th (North Midland) Division in France 1917. The colored cloth diamond sign denotes the unit and brigade.

Sergeant Heyes, DCM, photographed in July 1915. He wears an unofficial Trench Mortar trade badge on his lower right hand sleeve. The smaller official pattern of TM sign was issued to coincide with the creation of the TMB's in 1916.

Opposite
A private from the 12th Battalion, Kings Royal Rifle Corps with cloth '12 KRR' title and battle sign for 60th Brigade, 20th (Light) Division. Note also the worsted 'LG' Lewis Gunner and Marksman badges, long service good conduct chevron and the wound stripe.

Left: A 2nd Battalion, Manchester Regiment sergeant with a sewn on 'MANCHESTER' title above a red diamond that denotes the brigade and three yellow bars that denotes 'C' Company. The Battalion was part of the 32nd Division.

Opposite
Top left: 1/16th (Queen's Westminster Rifles) Battalion, London Regiment, 56th (London) Division lance corporal Lewis Gunner. Note the 'QWR' cloth sign and the wristwatch with mesh trench-guard.

Top right: 1/13th (Kensington) Battalion, London Regiment, 56th (London) Division lance corporals wearing cloth 'Kensington I' titles and brigade diamonds on the arms. Note the metal pioneer's trade badge.

Bottom left: A lance corporal from the 1/14th (London Scottish) Battalion, London Regiment with a cloth 'LONDON SCOTTISH' patch. As part of the 56th (London) Division this unit also wore the divisional sign of a red vertical sword on the back of the jacket.

Bottom right: A CSM from the 1/9th (Queen Victoria's Rifles) Battalion, London Regiment, 56th (London) Division. His cloth insignia comprises of a Best Shooting and Marksman's trade badge, a five-pointed TF Proficiency Star and 'QVR' cloth unit patch.

Buglers from the 1/18th (London Irish Rifles) Battalion, London Regiment, 47th (London) Division with slip-on 'LONDON IRISH' titles.

Welsh Regiment NCO's wearing the red Welsh dragon sign adopted by the 38th (Welsh) Division. The sign was worn on the left sleeve only, whilst on the right a scheme of shaped battle patches were worn to denote the brigade, and individual unit.

Army, Corps and Divisional Signs

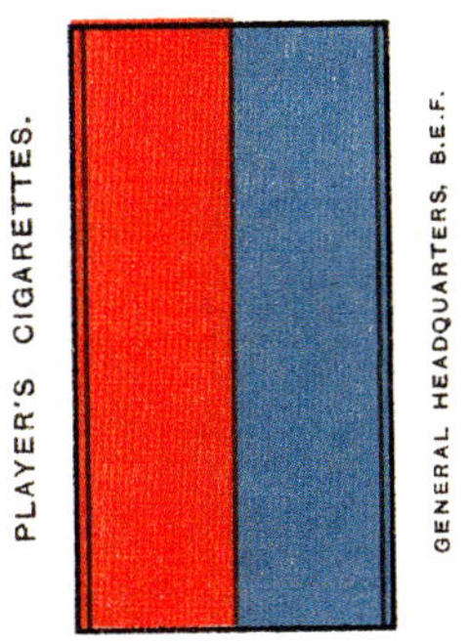

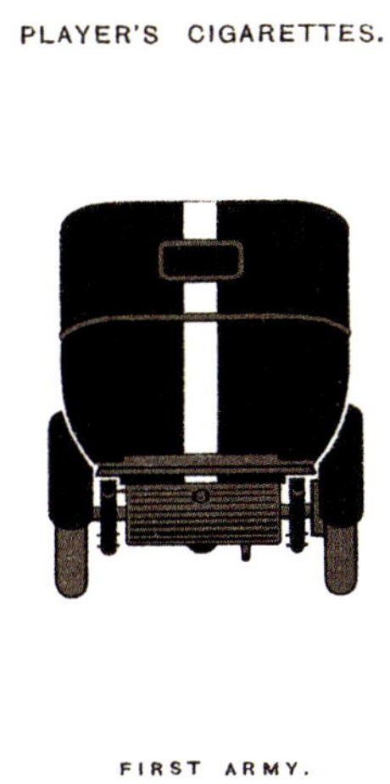

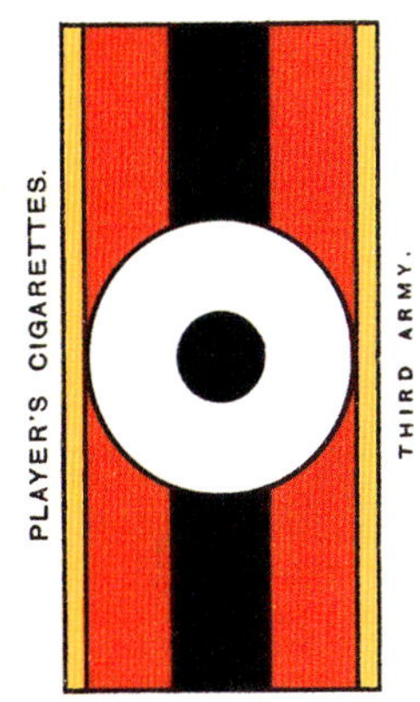

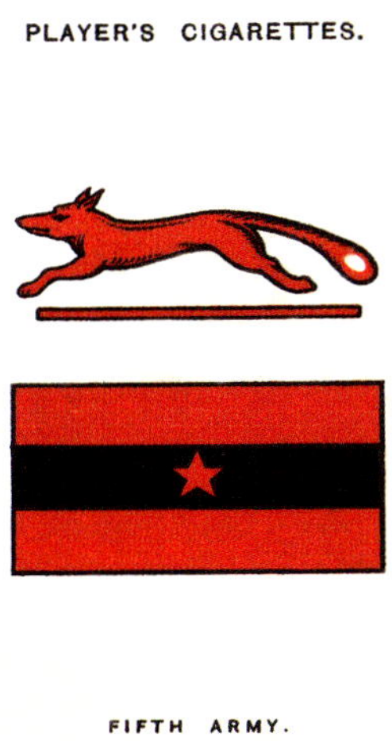

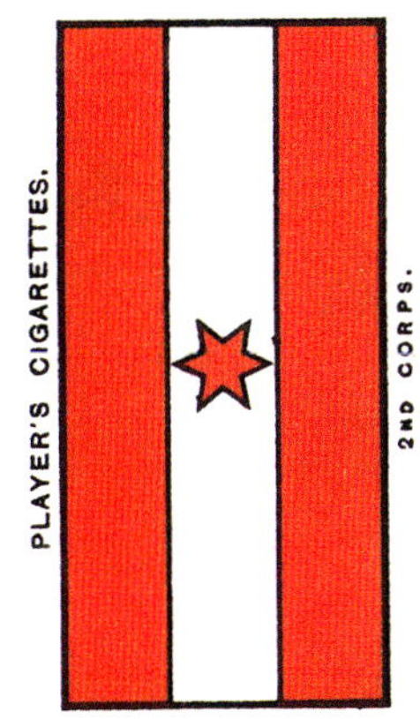

PLAYER'S CIGARETTES.
3RD CORPS.

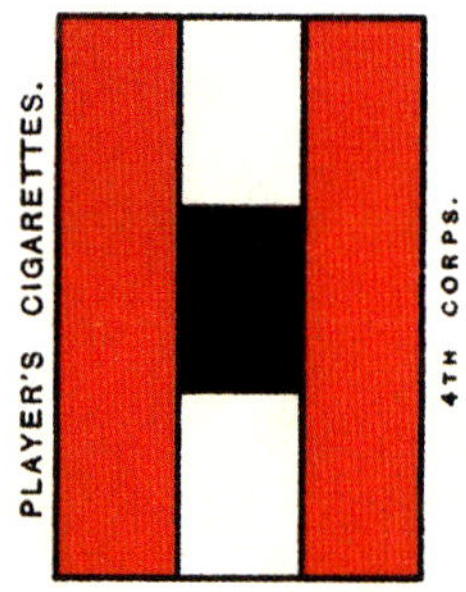
PLAYER'S CIGARETTES.
4TH CORPS.

PLAYER'S CIGARETTES.
5TH CORPS.

PLAYER'S CIGARETTES.
6TH CORPS.

PLAYER'S CIGARETTES.
7TH CORPS.

PLAYER'S CIGARETTES.
8TH CORPS.

PLAYER'S CIGARETTES.
9TH CORPS.

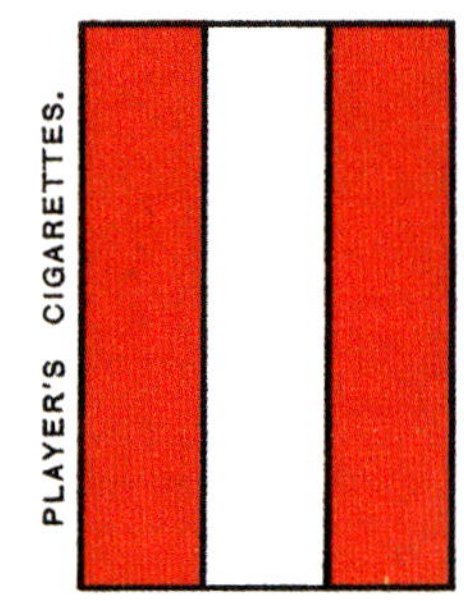
PLAYER'S CIGARETTES.
10TH CORPS.

PLAYER'S CIGARETTES.
11TH CORPS.

PLAYER'S CIGARETTES.
13TH CORPS.

PLAYER'S CIGARETTES.
14TH CORPS.

PLAYER'S CIGARETTES.
15TH CORPS.

PLAYER'S CIGARETTES.

17TH CORPS.

PLAYER'S CIGARETTES.

18TH CORPS.

PLAYER'S CIGARETTES

19TH CORPS

PLAYER'S CIGARETTES.

20TH CORPS.

PLAYER'S CIGARETTES.

21ST CORPS.

PLAYER'S CIGARETTES.

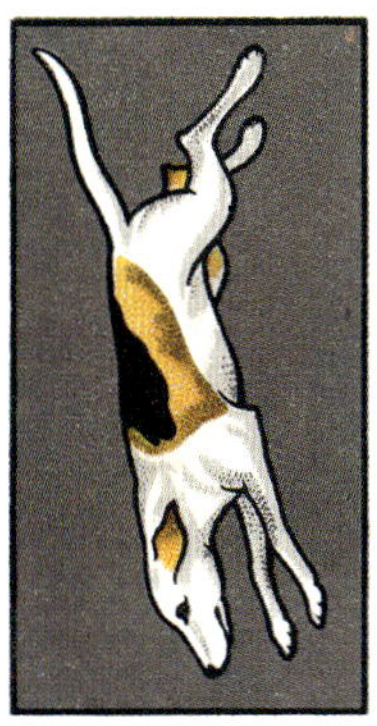

22ND CORPS.

PLAYER'S CIGARETTES.

DESERT
MOUNTED CORPS.

PLAYER'S CIGARETTES.

RUSSIAN RELIEF FORCE.

PLAYER'S CIGARETTES.

CAVALRY CORPS.

PLAYER'S CIGARETTES.

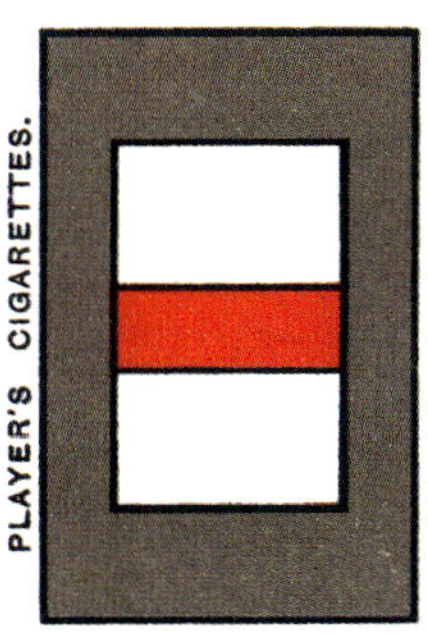

1ST CAVALRY DIVISION.

PLAYER'S CIGARETTES.

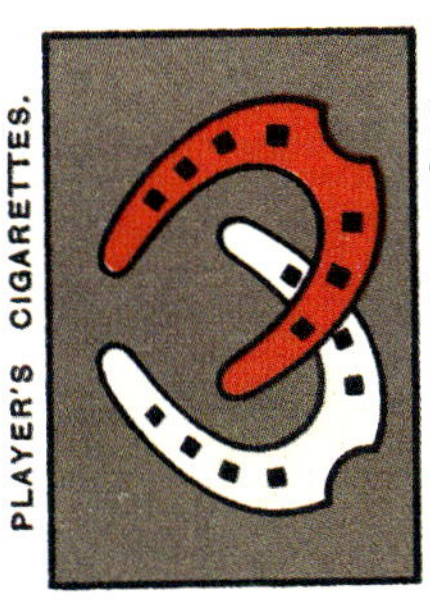

2ND CAVALRY DIVISION.

PLAYER'S CIGARETTES.

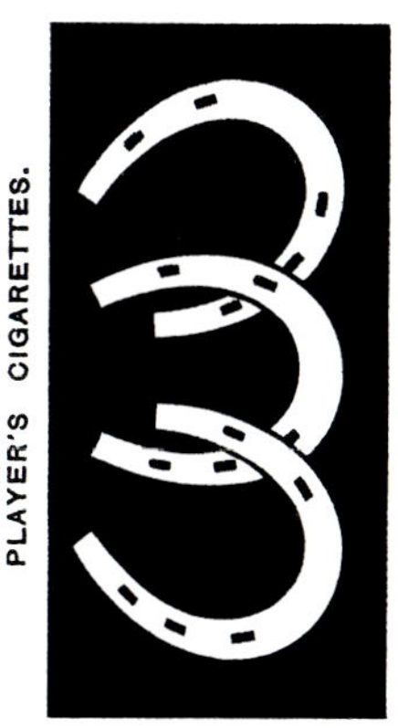

3RD CAVALRY DIVISION.

PLAYER'S CIGARETTES.
GUARDS DIVISION.

PLAYER'S CIGARETTES.
1ST DIVISION.

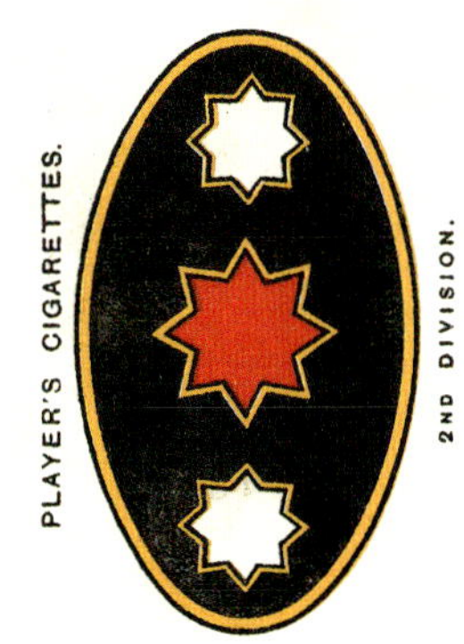
PLAYER'S CIGARETTES.
2ND DIVISION.

PLAYER'S CIGARETTES.
3RD DIVISION.

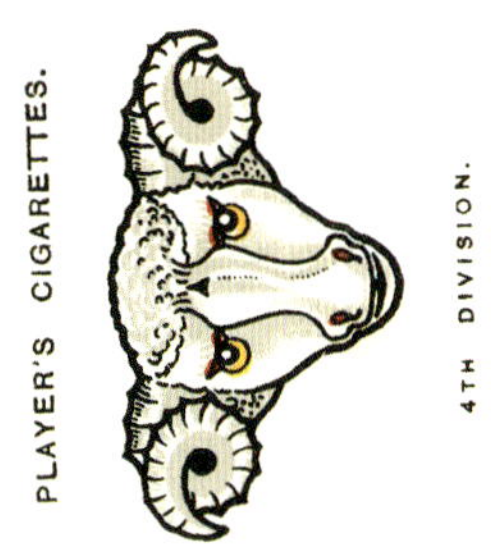
PLAYER'S CIGARETTES.
4TH DIVISION.

PLAYER'S CIGARETTES.
5TH DIVISION.

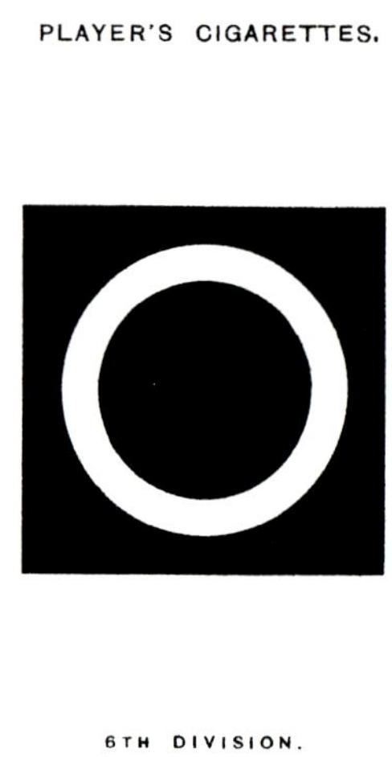
PLAYER'S CIGARETTES.
6TH DIVISION.

PLAYER'S CIGARETTES.
7TH DIVISION.

PLAYER'S CIGARETTES.
8TH DIVISION.

PLAYER'S CIGARETTES.
9TH DIVISION.

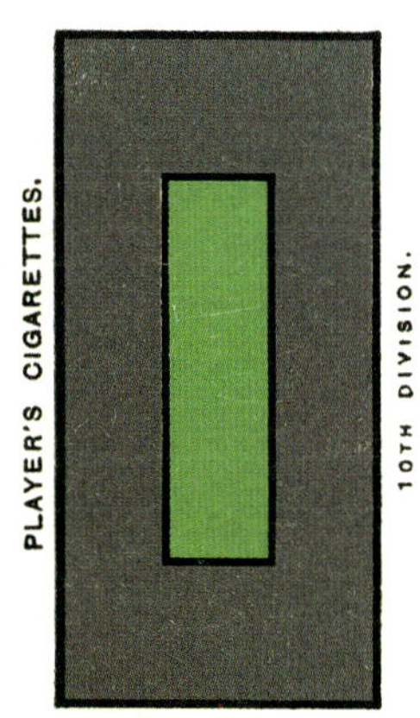
PLAYER'S CIGARETTES.
10TH DIVISION.

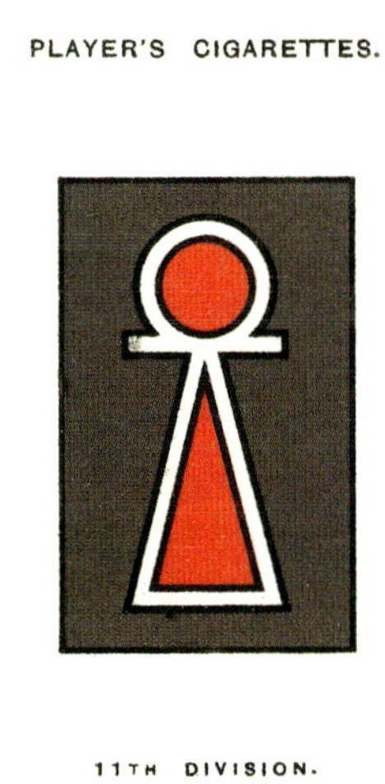
PLAYER'S CIGARETTES.
11TH DIVISION.

PLAYER'S CIGARETTES.

12TH DIVISION.

PLAYER'S CIGARETTES.

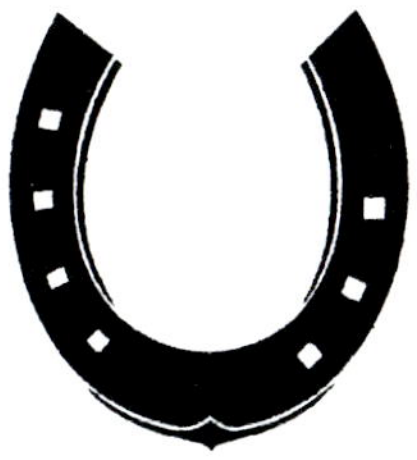

13TH DIVISION.

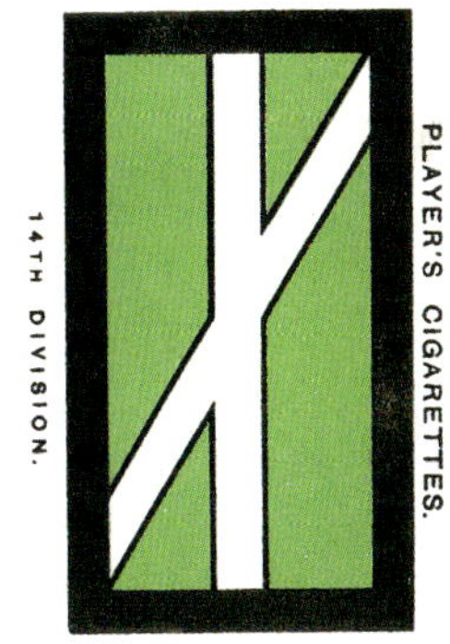

PLAYER'S CIGARETTES.

15TH DIVISION.

PLAYER'S CIGARETTES.

16TH DIVISION.

PLAYER'S CIGARETTES.

16TH DIVISION.

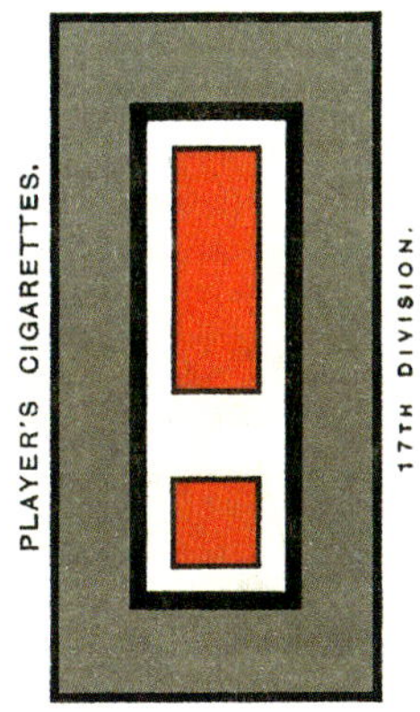

PLAYER'S CIGARETTES.

18TH DIVISION.

PLAYER'S CIGARETTES.

19TH DIVISION.

PLAYER'S CIGARETTES.

20TH DIVISION.

PLAYER'S CIGARETTES.

21ST DIVISION.

PLAYER'S CIGARETTES.

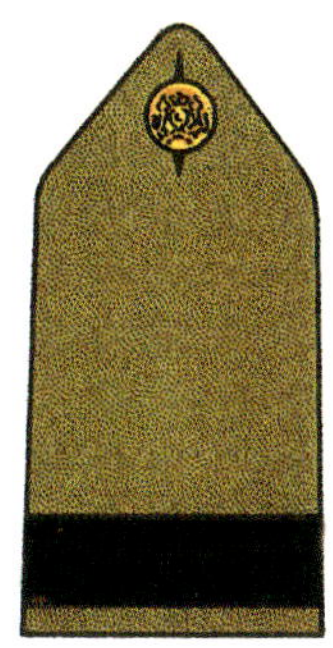

22ND DIVISION.

PLAYER'S CIGARETTES.

23RD DIVISION.

PLAYER'S CIGARETTES.

24TH DIVISION.

PLAYER'S CIGARETTES.

25TH DIVISION.

PLAYER'S CIGARETTES.

25TH DIVISION.

PLAYER'S CIGARETTES.

26TH DIVISION.

PLAYER'S CIGARETTES.

27TH DIVISION.

PLAYER'S CIGARETTES.

28TH DIVISION.

PLAYER'S CIGARETTES.

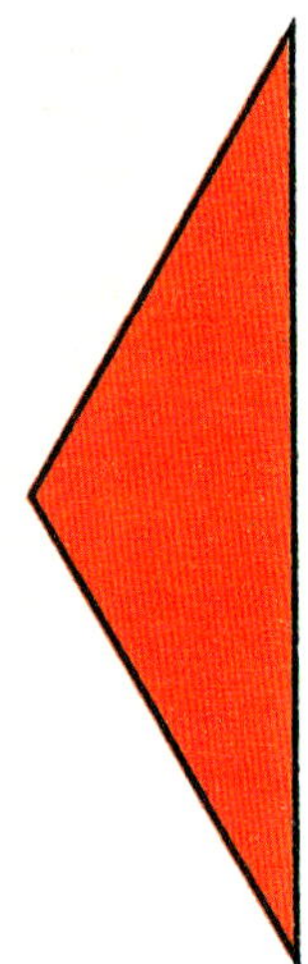

29TH DIVISION.

PLAYER'S CIGARETTES.

30TH DIVISION.

PLAYER'S CIGARETTES.

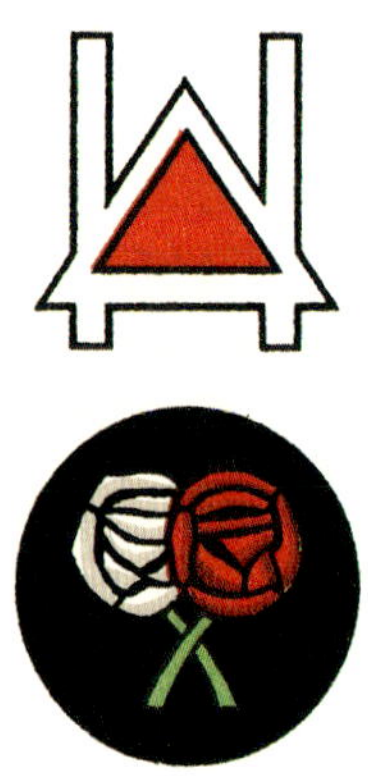

31ST DIVISION.

PLAYER'S CIGARETTES.

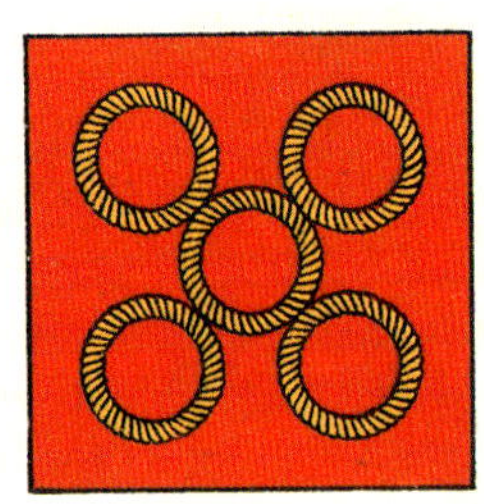

32ND DIVISION.

PLAYER'S CIGARETTES.

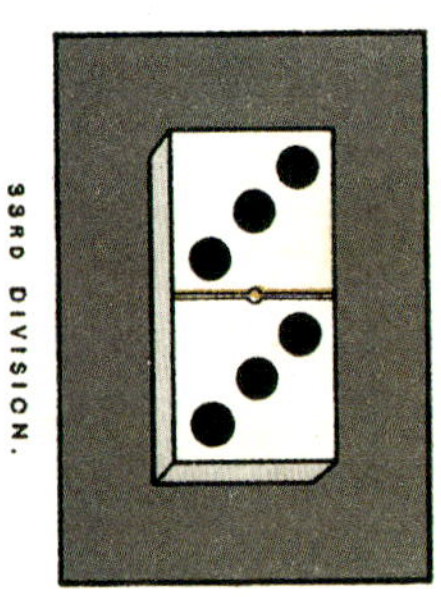

33RD DIVISION.

PLAYER'S CIGARETTES.

34TH DIVISION.

PLAYER'S CIGARETTES.

35TH DIVISION.

PLAYER'S CIGARETTES.

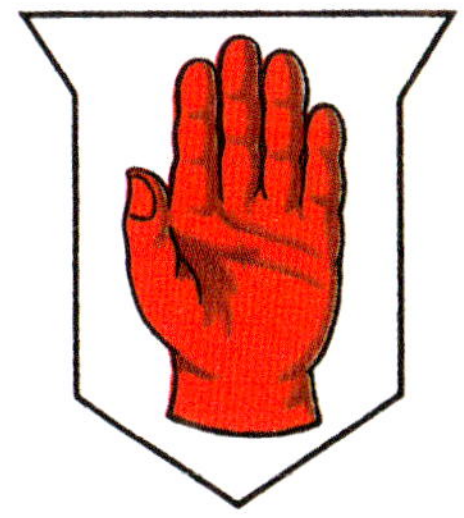

36TH DIVISION.

PLAYER'S CIGARETTES.

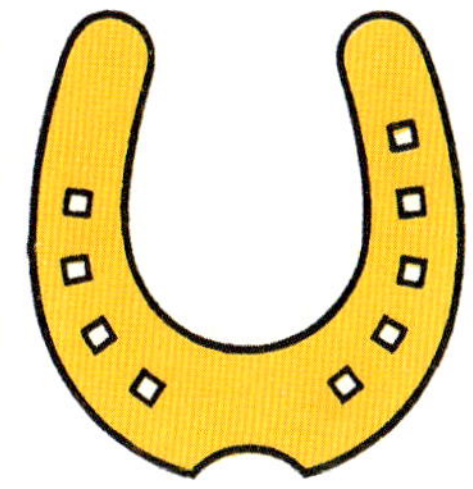

37TH DIVISION.

PLAYER'S CIGARETTES.

38TH DIVISION.

PLAYER'S CIGARETTES.

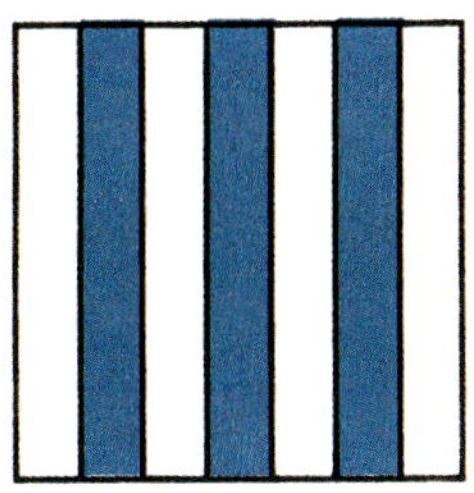

39TH DIVISION.

PLAYER'S CIGARETTES.

40TH DIVISION.

PLAYER'S CIGARETTES.

41ST DIVISION.

PLAYER'S CIGARETTES.

42ND DIVISION.

PLAYER'S CIGARETTES.

46TH DIVISION.

PLAYER'S CIGARETTES.

47TH DIVISION.

PLAYER'S CIGARETTES.

48TH DIVISION.

PLAYER'S CIGARETTES.

49TH DIVISION.

PLAYER'S CIGARETTES.

50TH DIVISION.

PLAYER'S CIGARETTES.

51ST DIVISION.

PLAYER'S CIGARETTES.

52ND DIVISION.

PLAYER'S CIGARETTES.

53RD DIVISION.

PLAYER'S CIGARETTES.

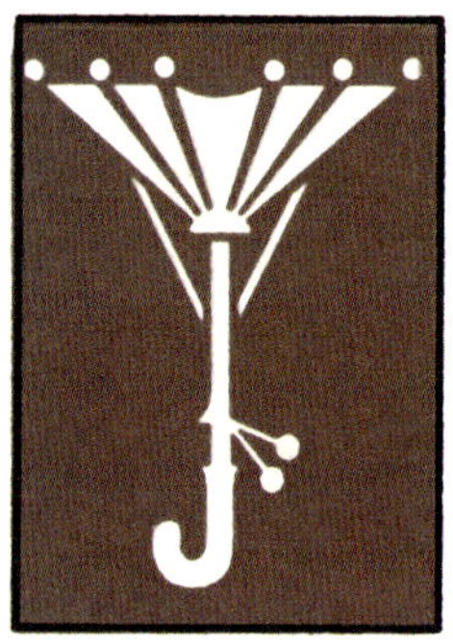

54TH DIVISION.

PLAYER'S CIGARETTES.

55TH DIVISION.

PLAYER'S CIGARETTES.

56TH DIVISION.

PLAYER'S CIGARETTES.

57TH DIVISION.

PLAYER'S CIGARETTES.

58TH DIVISION.

PLAYER'S CIGARETTES.

59TH DIVISION.

PLAYER'S CIGARETTES.

60TH DIVISION.

PLAYER'S CIGARETTES.
61ST DIVISION.

PLAYER'S CIGARETTES.
62ND DIVISION.

PLAYER'S CIGARETTES.
63RD DIVISION.

PLAYER'S CIGARETTES.
65TH DIVISION.

PLAYER'S CIGARETTES.
66TH DIVISION.

PLAYER'S CIGARETTES.
67TH DIVISION.

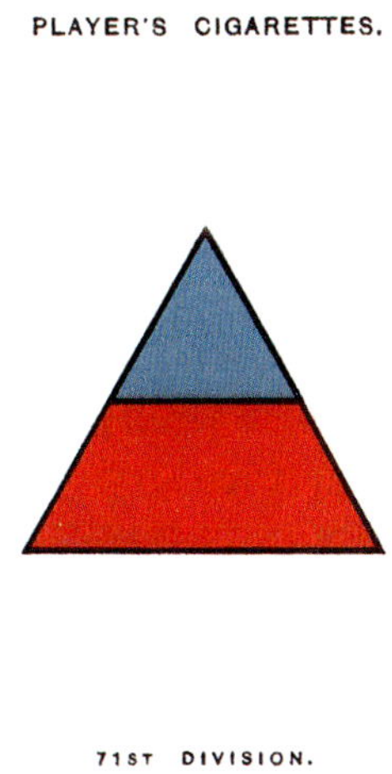
PLAYER'S CIGARETTES.
71ST DIVISION.

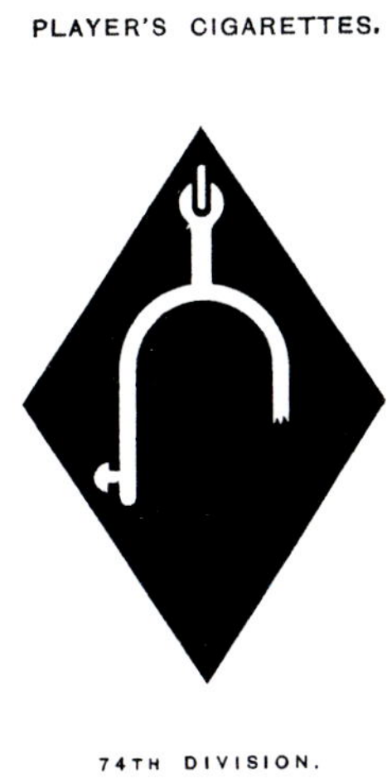
PLAYER'S CIGARETTES.
74TH DIVISION.

PLAYER'S CIGARETTES.
75TH DIVISION.

PLAYER'S CIGARETTES.
1ST (INDIAN) CORPS.

PLAYER'S CIGARETTES.
SHUMRAN
1917
DIYALAH
3RD (INDIAN) CORPS.

PLAYER'S CIGARETTES.
17TH (INDIAN) DIVISION.

PLAYER'S CIGARETTES.

18TH (INDIAN) DIVISION.

PLAYER'S CIGARETTES.

14TH (INDIAN) DIVISION.

PLAYER'S CIGARETTES.

15TH (INDIAN) DIVISION.

PLAYER'S CIGARETTES.

7TH (INDIAN)
CAVALRY BRIGADE.

PLAYER'S CIGARETTES.

6TH (INDIAN)
CAVALRY BRIGADE.

PLAYER'S CIGARETTES.

11TH CAVALRY BRIGADE.

PLAYER'S CIGARETTES.

EUPHRATES DEFENCES.

PLAYER'S CIGARETTES.

PERSIAN LINES OF COMMUNICATION.

PLAYER'S CIGARETTES.

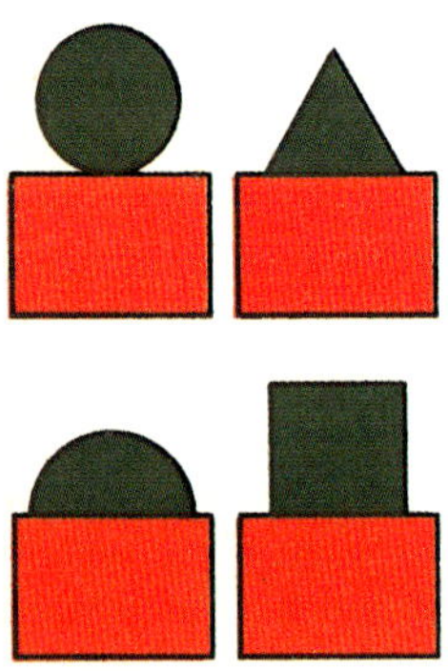

1ST CANADIAN DIVISION.
1ST INFANTRY BRIGADE.

PLAYER'S CIGARETTES.

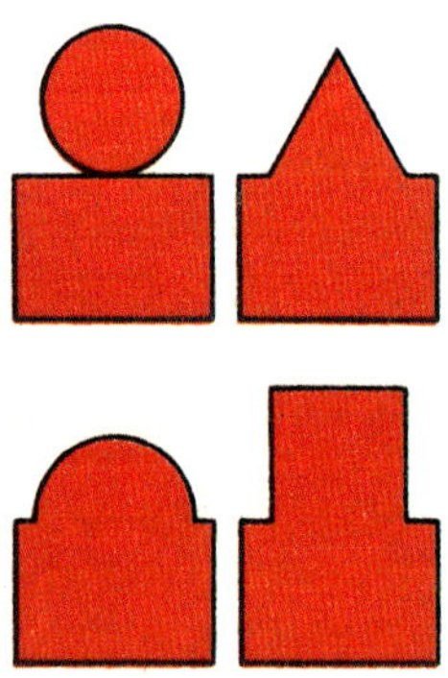

1ST CANADIAN DIVISION.
2ND INFANTRY BRIGADE.

PLAYER'S CIGARETTES.

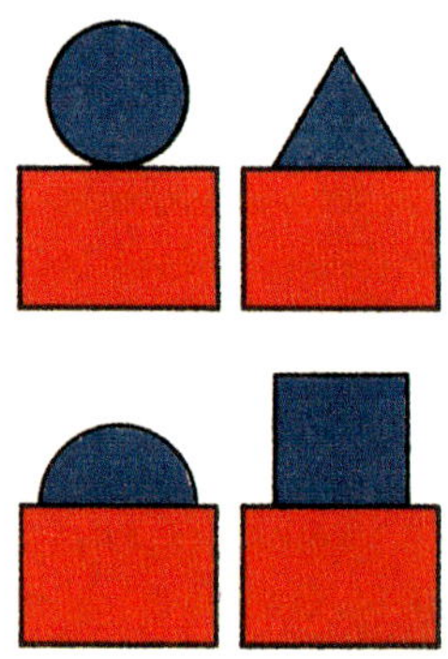

1ST CANADIAN DIVISION.
3RD INFANTRY BRIGADE.

PLAYER'S CIGARETTES.

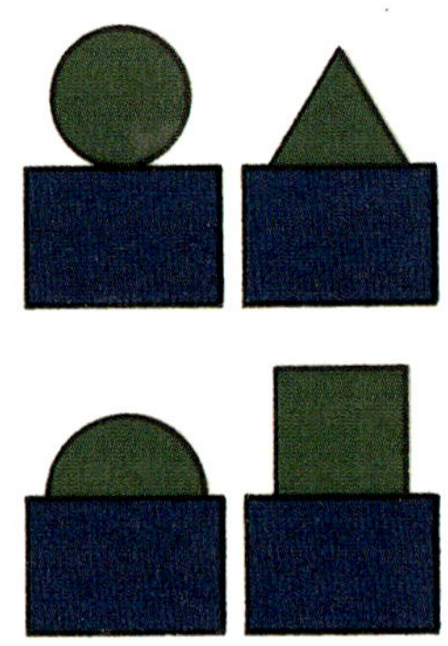

2ND CANADIAN DIVISION.
4TH INFANTRY BRIGADE.

PLAYER'S CIGARETTES.

2ND CANADIAN DIVISION.
5TH INFANTRY BRIGADE.

PLAYER'S CIGARETTES.

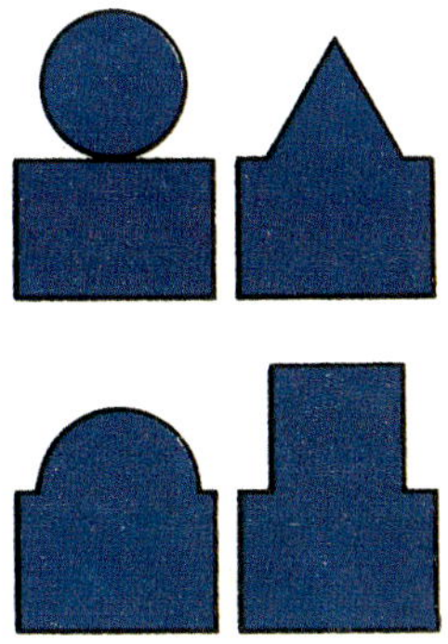

2ND CANADIAN DIVISION.
6TH INFANTRY BRIGADE.

PLAYER'S CIGARETTES.

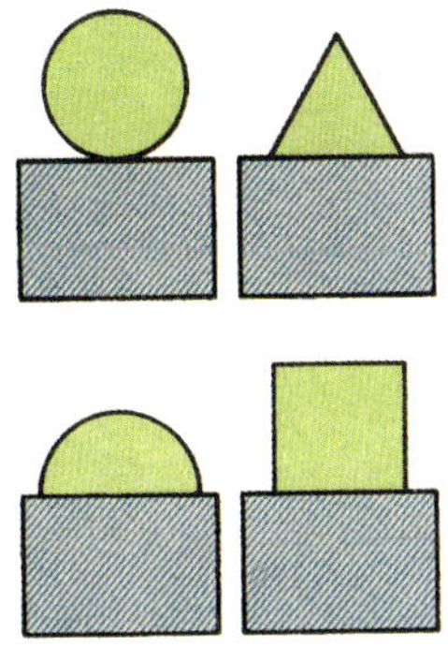

3RD CANADIAN DIVISION.
7TH INFANTRY BRIGADE.

PLAYER'S CIGARETTES.

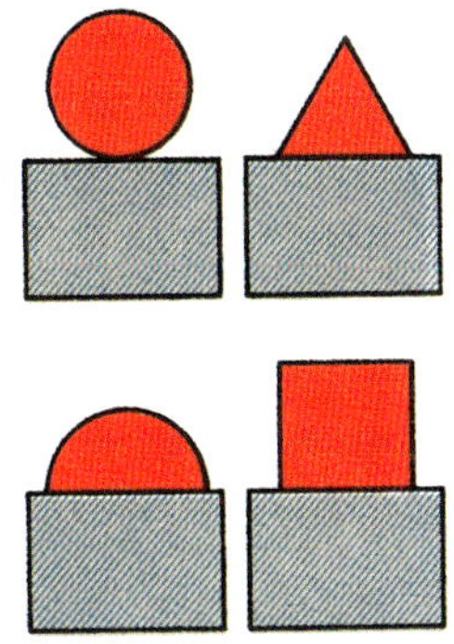

3RD CANADIAN DIVISION.
8TH INFANTRY BRIGADE.

PLAYER'S CIGARETTES.

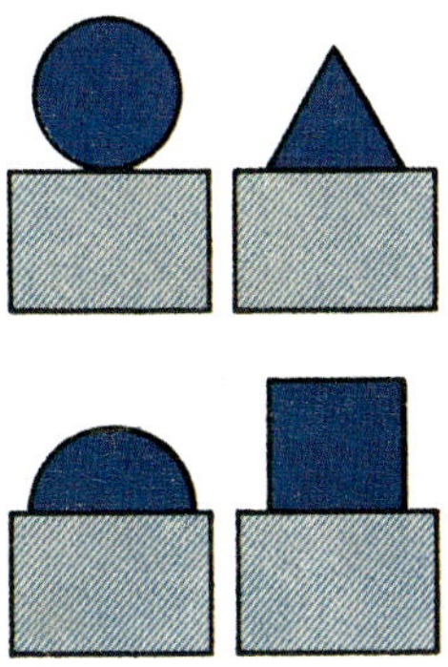

3RD CANADIAN DIVISION.
9TH INFANTRY BRIGADE.

PLAYER'S CIGARETTES.

4TH CANADIAN DIVISION.
10TH INFANTRY BRIGADE.

PLAYER'S CIGARETTES.

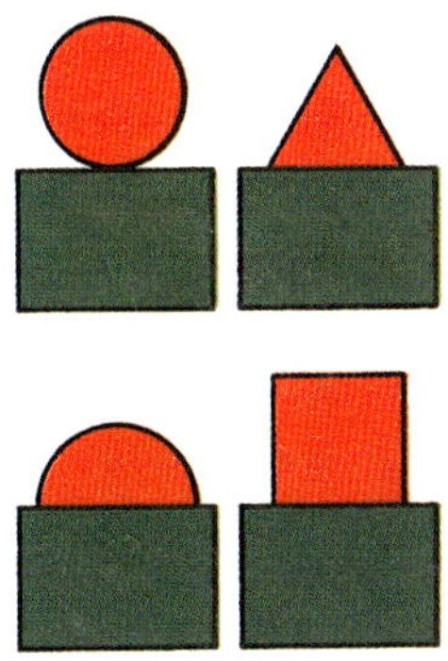

4TH CANADIAN DIVISION.
11TH INFANTRY BRIGADE.

PLAYER'S CIGARETTES.

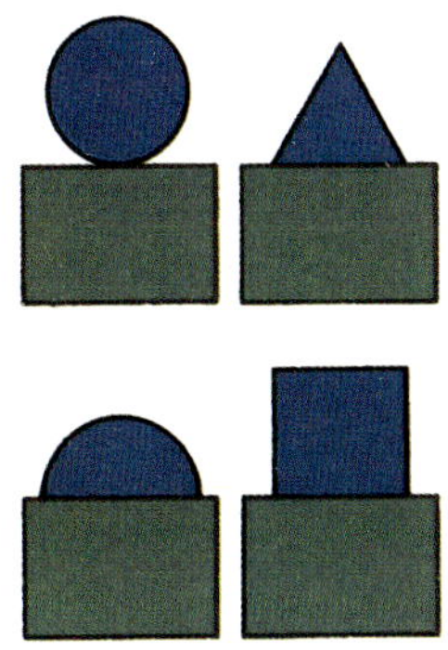

4TH CANADIAN DIVISION.
12TH INFANTRY BRIGADE.

PLAYER'S CIGARETTES.

NEW ZEALAND DIVISION.

PLAYER'S CIGARETTES.

AUSTRALIAN CORPS.

PLAYER'S CIGARETTES.

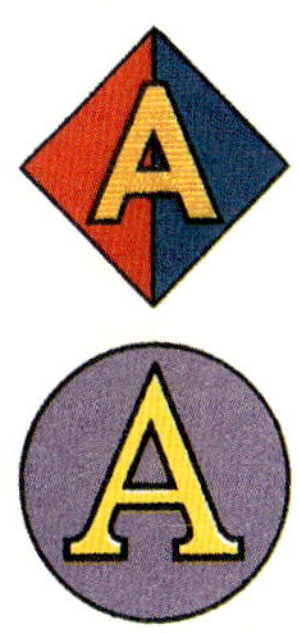

THE ANZAC EMBLEM.

PLAYER'S CIGARETTES.

DIVISIONAL SIGN.

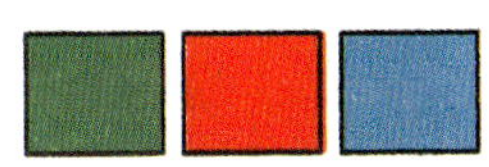

1ST 2ND 3RD
BRIGADE SIGNS.

1ST AUSTRALIAN DIVISION.

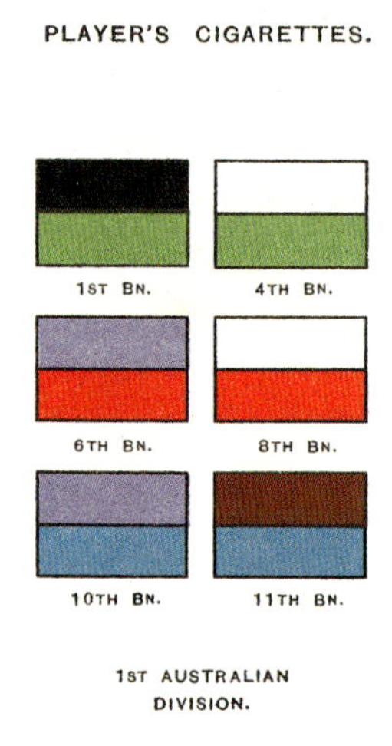
PLAYER'S CIGARETTES.
1ST BN.
4TH BN.
6TH BN.
8TH BN.
10TH BN.
11TH BN.
1ST AUSTRALIAN DIVISION.

PLAYER'S CIGARETTES.
DIVISIONAL SIGN.
5TH
6TH
7TH
BRIGADE SIGNS.
2ND AUSTRALIAN DIVISION.

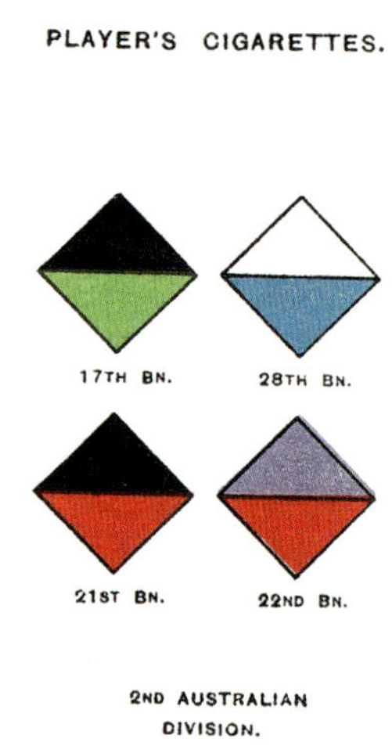
PLAYER'S CIGARETTES.
17TH BN.
28TH BN.
21ST BN.
22ND BN.
2ND AUSTRALIAN DIVISION.

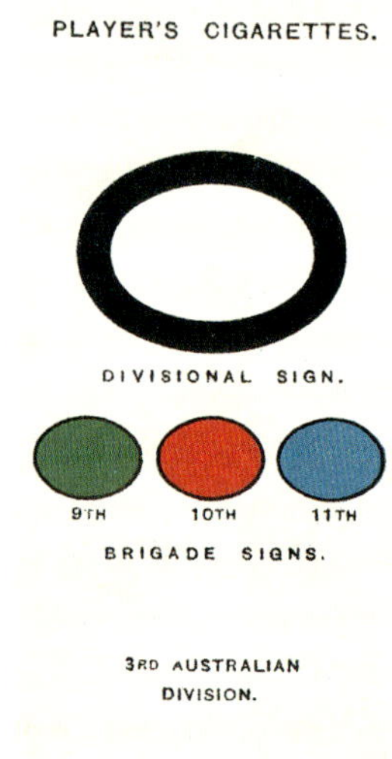
PLAYER'S CIGARETTES.
DIVISIONAL SIGN.
9TH
10TH
11TH
BRIGADE SIGNS.
3RD AUSTRALIAN DIVISION.

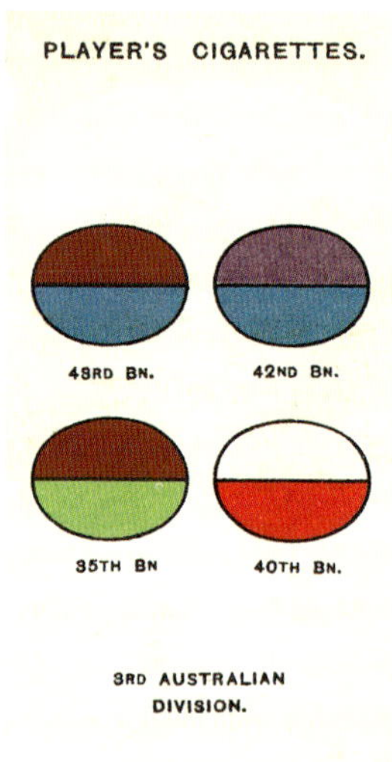
PLAYER'S CIGARETTES.
43RD BN.
42ND BN.
35TH BN
40TH BN.
3RD AUSTRALIAN DIVISION.

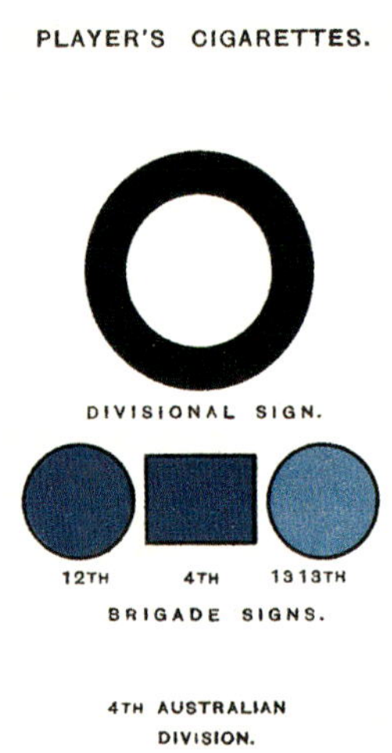
PLAYER'S CIGARETTES.
DIVISIONAL SIGN.
12TH
4TH
1313TH
BRIGADE SIGNS.
4TH AUSTRALIAN DIVISION.

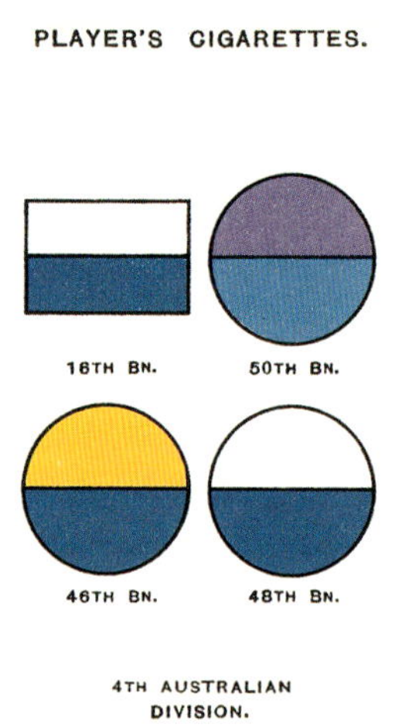
PLAYER'S CIGARETTES.
16TH BN.
50TH BN.
46TH BN.
48TH BN.
4TH AUSTRALIAN DIVISION.

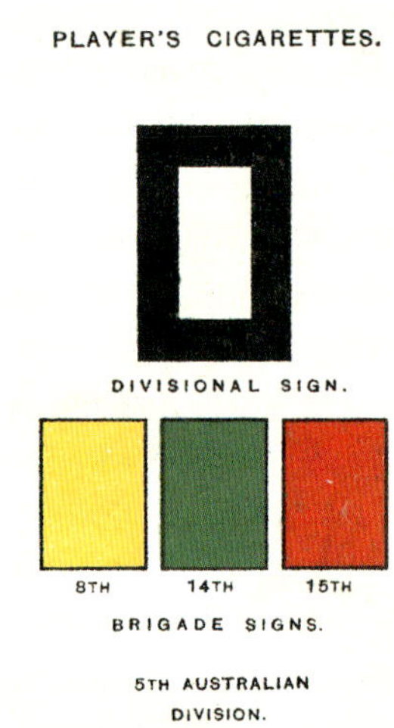
PLAYER'S CIGARETTES.
DIVISIONAL SIGN.
8TH
14TH
15TH
BRIGADE SIGNS.
5TH AUSTRALIAN DIVISION.

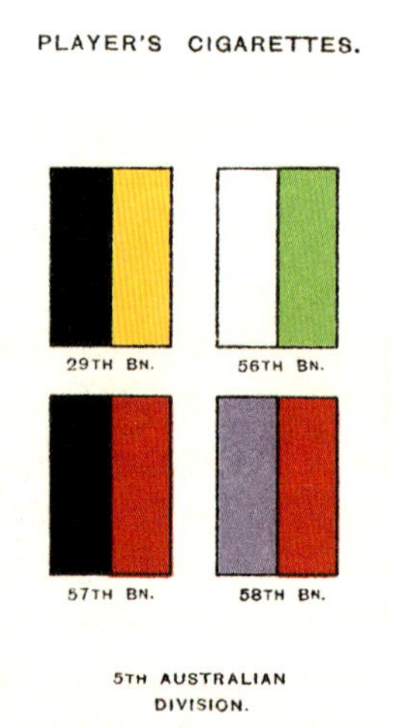
PLAYER'S CIGARETTES.
29TH BN.
56TH BN.
57TH BN.
58TH BN.
5TH AUSTRALIAN DIVISION.

PLAYER'S CIGARETTES.
AUSTRALIAN FLYING CORPS.

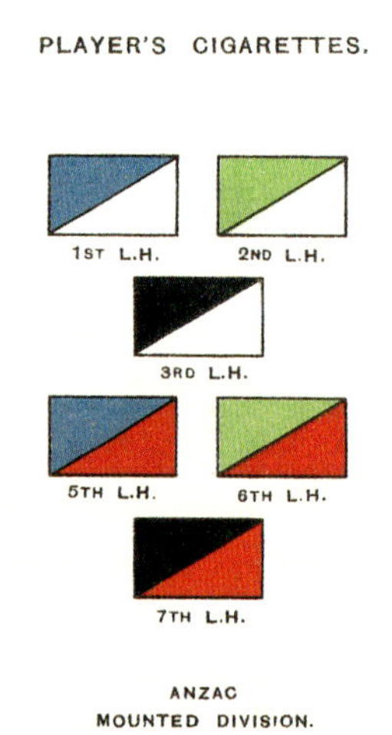
PLAYER'S CIGARETTES.
1ST L.H.
2ND L.H.
3RD L.H.
5TH L.H.
6TH L.H.
7TH L.H.
ANZAC MOUNTED DIVISION.

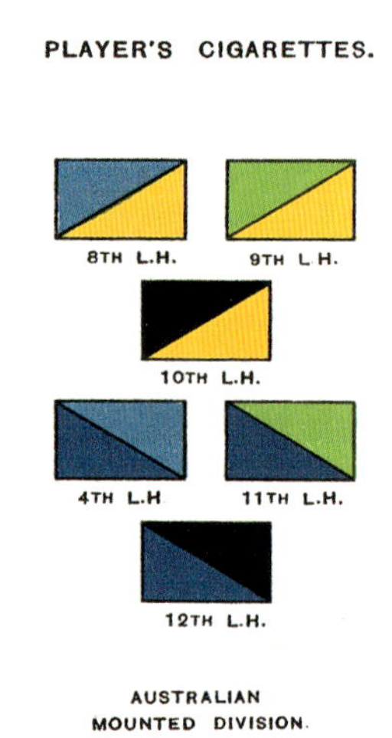
PLAYER'S CIGARETTES.
8TH L.H.
9TH L.H.
10TH L.H.
4TH L.H
11TH L.H.
12TH L.H.
AUSTRALIAN MOUNTED DIVISION.

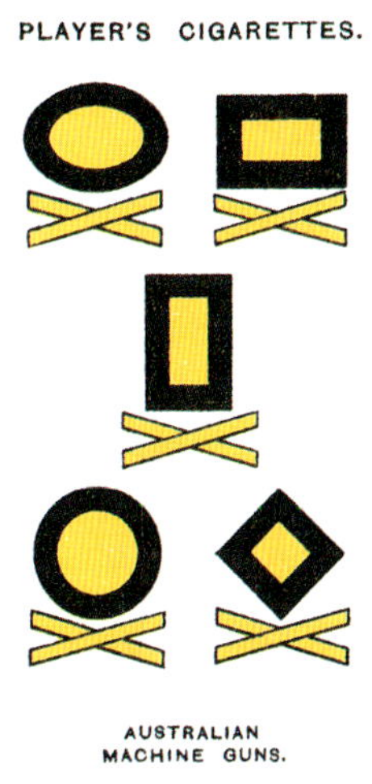
PLAYER'S CIGARETTES.
AUSTRALIAN MACHINE GUNS.

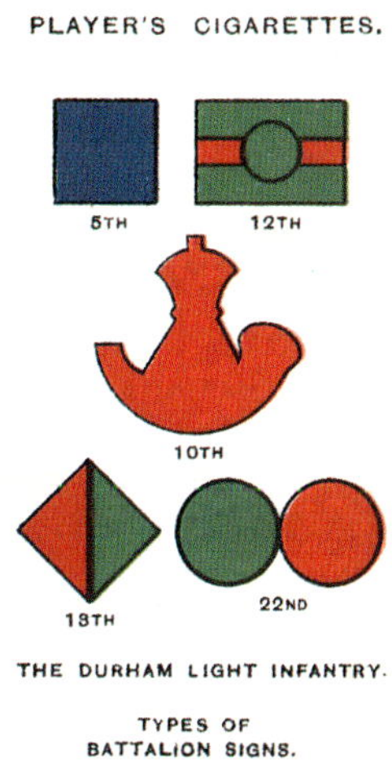
PLAYER'S CIGARETTES.
5TH
12TH
10TH
13TH
22ND
THE DURHAM LIGHT INFANTRY.
TYPES OF BATTALION SIGNS.

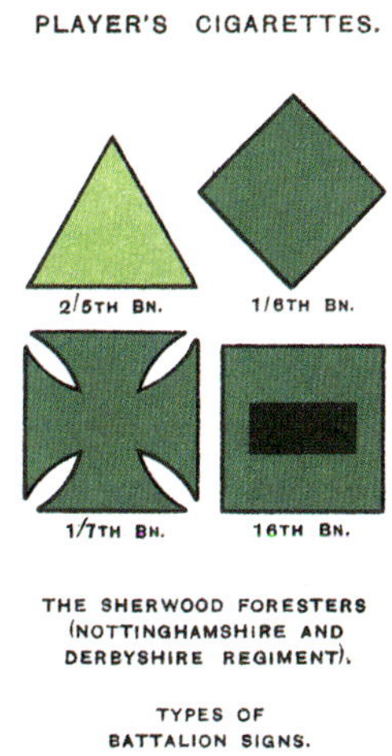
PLAYER'S CIGARETTES.
2/5TH BN.
1/6TH BN.
1/7TH BN.
16TH BN.
THE SHERWOOD FORESTERS (NOTTINGHAMSHIRE AND DERBYSHIRE REGIMENT).
TYPES OF BATTALION SIGNS.

PLAYER'S CIGARETTES.
2ND
1/5TH 1/6TH 1/7TH 1/8TH
2/5TH 2/6TH 2/7TH 2/8TH
THE WEST YORKSHIRE REGIMENT. (THE PRINCE OF WALES'S OWN).
TYPES OF BATTALION SIGNS.

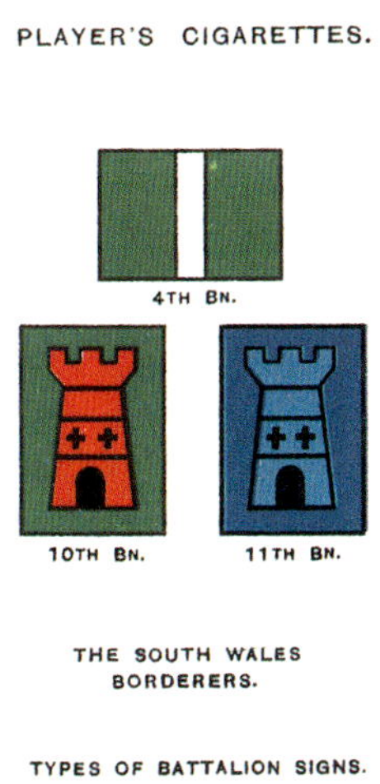
PLAYER'S CIGARETTES.
4TH BN.
10TH BN.
11TH BN.
THE SOUTH WALES BORDERERS.
TYPES OF BATTALION SIGNS.

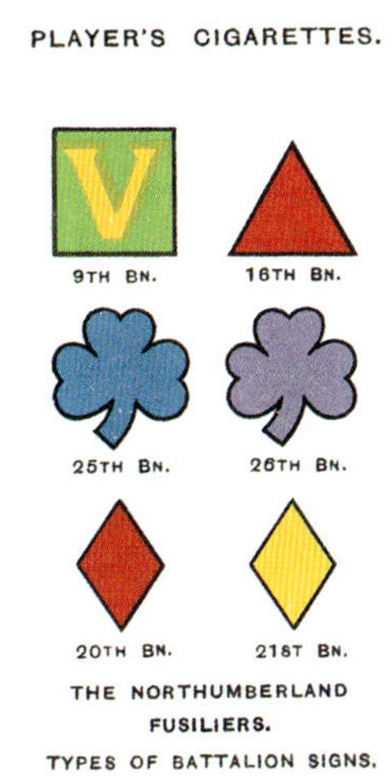
PLAYER'S CIGARETTES.
V
9TH BN.
16TH BN.
25TH BN.
26TH BN.
20TH BN.
21ST BN.
THE NORTHUMBERLAND FUSILIERS.
TYPES OF BATTALION SIGNS.

PLAYER'S CIGARETTES.
OFFICERS, 1ST BN.
RANGERS
1ST BN.
2ND BN.
12TH LONDON REGIMENT (RANGERS).
TYPES OF BATTALION SIGNS.

PLAYER'S CIGARETTES.
1ST BATTALION.
10TH BN.
14TH BN.
THE HAMPSHIRE REGIMENT.
TYPES OF BATTALION SIGNS.

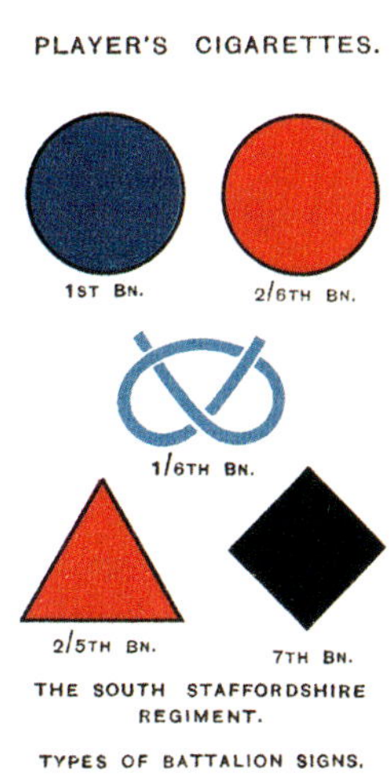
PLAYER'S CIGARETTES.
1ST BN.
2/6TH BN.
1/6TH BN.
2/5TH BN.
7TH BN.
THE SOUTH STAFFORDSHIRE REGIMENT.
TYPES OF BATTALION SIGNS.

PLAYER'S CIGARETTES.
MACHINE GUN CORPS.

Bibliography

Barthorpe, M., *The Old Contemptibles*, London, 1989.
Bull, S., *World War One British Army*, London, 1998.
Chappell, M., *British Infantry Equipments, 1808-1908*, London, 1980.
— *British Infantry Equipments, 1908-1980*, London, 1980.
— *British Cavalry Equipments, 1800-1941*, London, 1983.
— *British Battle Insignia, 1914-1918*, London, 1986.
— *The British Army in World War 1 (1) 1914-16*, London, 2003.
Cormack, A., *British Air Forces, 1914-1918 (1)*, London, 2000.
— *British Air Forces, 1914-1918 (2)*, London, 2002.
Easterly, W. M., *The Belgian Rattlesnake,* Ontario, Canada, 1998.
Goldsmith, D., *The Grand Old Lady of No Man's Land*, Ontario, Canada, 1994.
James, E.A., *British Regiments, 1914-1918*, London, 1978.
Kipling, A.L., and King, H.L., *Head-Dress Badges of the British Army*, London, 1978.
Pegler, M., *British Tommy, 1914-1918*, London, 1996.
Saunders, A., *Weapons of the Trench War 1914-1918*, Stroud, 1999.
— *Dominating the Enemy*, Stroud, 2000.
Skennerton, I., *The British Service Lee*, Margate, Australia, 1982.
— *An Introduction to British Grenades*, Margate, Australia, 1988
Westlake, R.A., *Kitchener's Army – A Pictorial History*, Kent, 1989.
British Territorial Units, 1914-1918, London, 1991.
Wheeler-Holohan, V., *Divisional and Other Signs*, London, 1920.

The above list is in no way intended to be exclusive and is certainly not intended as a comment on the value of any books I have omitted to mention.